AVKO Sequential Spelling 4 for Home Study Learning

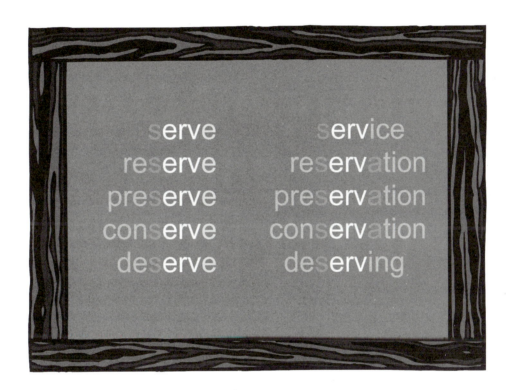

by

Don McCabe

AVKO Educational Research Foundation

Dedication

This book is dedicated to:
All the members of the AVKO Dyslexia Research Foundation,
but especially to the memory of one of its first members,

Mary Clair Scott
without whose work and devotion to the cause of literacy,
the AVKO Foundation might never have gotten off the ground,

Betty June Szilagyi
who was my first and by far my most important teacher,

Devorah Wolf
without whose encouragement and commitment
to the ideals of AVKO
this edition would not be possible,

Ann, Robert, and Linda McCabe
all of whom have sacrificed much of their time and energy
helping AVKO grow
as well as all those friends and relatives
who have been a source of encouragement.

May this book help you to help others improve their abilities to read and write.

Publisher's Cataloging in Publication Data
McCabe, Donald J.
1. Spelling—Miscellanea 2. Reading—Miscellanea 3. Curriculum—Miscellanea 4. Literacy.
Library of Congress Subject Headings: Spelling, Reading, Curriculum
Library of Congress Classification Number: LB1050.2F79
Library of Congress Card Number: To be determined
Dewey Decimal Classification Number 428.4
ISBN: 1-56400-964-5

The Basic Concepts of Teaching Spelling by Word Families

You may have used the concept of rhyming words that have the same letter endings to help your students learn to read. For example, you may have introduced the word *at*, then also shared *cat*, *bat*, *sat*, and maybe even *scat*. Unfortunately, you have never had any source book for finding all the rhyming words with the same spelling patterns. [NOTE: In the latest academic jargon word families are now called "rimes." The consonants, consonant blends, and digraphs that precede the word family (or rime) are now called onsets. Use whatever term you wish with your students. In this book, I generally use the terms *base*

or *word family* rather than the new jargon word "rime."]

The Patterns of English Spelling (formerly *Word Families Plus*) is now available to be used as a source book so that you can teach any word family. This is not just a simple collection of word lists. This book consists of complete patterns to help your students (and quite often parents and teachers!) see patterns that exist and to lock in on those patterns with their "computer" brains. For example, I believe that if you can teach your students (or anyone) the word *at*, you can also teach them:

bat	bats	batted	batting		
cat	cats				
scat	scats				
flat	flats	flatted	flatting		
pat	pats	patted	patting		
spat	spats				
mat	mats	matted	matting		
rat	rats	ratted	ratting		
hatter	batters	battered	battering	battery	batteries
flatter	flatters	flattered	flattering	flattery	
matter	matters	mattered	mattering		
battle	battles	battled	battling		
cattle					
rattle	rattles	rattled	rattling		

OR, for a more sophisticated example, from the word **act** you can build:

act	acts	acted	acting	active	action
fact	facts				
tract	tracts				traction
attract	attracts	attracted	attracting	attractive	attraction
distract	distracts	distracted	distracting		distraction
extract	extracts	extracted	extracting	extractive	extraction
subtract	subtracts	subtracted	subtracting		subtraction
contract	contracts	contracted	contracting		contraction

Perhaps the most important difference between the traditional approach to spelling and the AVKO (**A**udio-**V**isual-**K**inesthetic-**O**ral) approach is that we use tests as a **learning** device and **not** as a method of **evaluation**. I believe that the natural method of learning is learning from mistakes, and that is why I want students to correct their own mistakes **when** they make them—so they can learn from them.

We developed the *AVKO Sequential Spelling Tests* to utilize the word family approach sequentially and to apply the very simple techniques of having students correct their own mistakes **when** they make them—not hours, days, or even weeks later.

Use a Dry Erase Board or Something Similar to Give AVKO Sequential Spelling Tests

---

The First Day

On your first day of using Sequential Spelling 4, share with your students:

I have some good news and some bad news. First the bad news. Today and every day until we finish this book, we are going to have a spelling test. The good news is that each one of you will correct your own paper. But before we start, I want each of you to take out a sheet of paper and put your name on it. Did you spell your name correctly? Good. That's my first test. My next test is like a doctor's test. It's not for a

grade so don't worry about it. Okay? Now write the following sentence:

We have some unfinished business to take care of.

If any of your students shows signs of struggling with the sentence, just ask them to try to spell the word *unfinished* only. If they still find it difficult to put down anything, ask them to just put down—in any order—some of the letters that might be in the word *unfinished*.

Now collect their papers.

On the 4th day, you will be able to demonstrate that your students who couldn't spell *unfinished* on the first day were able to correctly spell it without ever having seen or studied the word. And remember that according to Harry Greene's *The New Iowa Spelling Scale* (1954) only 21% of all public school 4rd graders can be expected to spell the word *finished.* Statistics are not available on the word *unfinished.* Even those who may miss the word will have a spelling much closer to the correct spelling than they did on the first day. We will expect that you will point that out to your students on the 4th day.

If your students have their own copy of the *AVKO Student Response Book for Sequential Spelling*, have them open their books to page 3. Note the location of Day 1. It is in the *middle* column of page 3. Day 2 is in the middle column on page 5. Day 3 is in the middle column on page 7. Day 4 is in the middle column on page 9, and so forth. Please note the AVKO motto on the bottom of these pages:

Mistakes are Opportunities to Learn

The reason for this arrangement is to prevent students from copying the base word that they had the day before and then just adding the -s, -ed, or -ing ending as the case may be. Just as students don't learn by copying from others, they don't learn by copying from themselves.

> If your students don't have a Student Response Book, have them use a notebook with single sheets of paper. Use one sheet for each day's spelling lesson.

● *In the column marked 1st day/Lesson 1, please write the word "**freakish**" as in: "We were involved in a **freakish** accident. **freakish**.*

*Now, I want every one of you to try. At least guess what letters **freakish** begins with. If you don't get it right, it's no big deal! So you erase it and write it right. Isn't that why erasers are put on the ends of pencils?*

While your students are attempting to write the word **freakish**, there may be some rubber necks or elastic eyeballs in action. This is not the time to jump on one of your students for doing it, but it is the time to ask them how much they are going to learn from someone else's mistakes. Tell them once again that they are correcting their own papers. Try to impress upon them that it doesn't make any sense to cheat.

After your students have attempted writing *freakish*, you now ask your students:

What are the first two letters in **freakish**?

Most will shout out, "F, R!" Now, you show on the dry erase board just the letters f and r. Now you ask what the last three letters of **freakish** are. Again, there will be shouts, "I-S-H". Then ask what three

letters are used to spell the middle sound of **freakish**. Congratulate any of your students who said "I-E-K,", "E-E-K," or even "E-I-K" KAY" because these are intelligent misspellings. The sound "*EE'k*" can be spelled those ways. In fact, "EE'k" can even be spelled -ique or -ic(!) as in *unique* and *chic*. The words *week*, *shriek*, and *sheik* can be used to illustrate that point. On the dry erase board you now show the *–eak* in black and then write ish in green to contrast with either red or green *fr* and the black *eak*. Have each child check his spelling with yours. Have them use their erasers and write it right.

Depending upon the age of your students and their attitudes, you may try to get them to spell aloud the word with you as they trace over their correct spelling. In other words, by hearing the word (**A**udio), seeing the word (**V**isual), writing the word (**K**inesthetic), and saying the word (**O**ral), the students are using a multi-sensory approach to learning that research has demonstrated is a powerful method. On the dry erase board you now show the -*as*. (It really doesn't matter what color you use for the A and the S. I personally like to use green for the word family patterns to contrast later on with the black *beginning letters*.)

Depending upon the age of your students and their attitudes, you may try to get them to spell aloud the word with you (the oral channel) as they trace over their corrected spelling (the kinesthetic channel).

Then you give the second word. **ticklish**. *Most little students are very, very* **ticklish**. **ticklish**. Each student tries to spell the word. You write **t** in green, **ickl** in black, **ish** in green. Some students may ask why there isn't an e after the letter l because there is one in the word *tickle*. Congratulate them for making an intelligent

6

error. Yes, you would think we would just add -ish to the word *tickle* to get *tickleish* (sic). However, we drop the "silent" letter e when we add a suffix that starts with a vowel.

The third word is **bluish**. *They painted the walls a sort of* **bluish** *color.* **bluish**. Again we find that the "silent" e is dropped.

Number 4 is **purplish**. *At least they didn't paint the walls some offbeat* **purplish** *color.* **purplish**.

As you go through the procedure with **purplish**, we recommend that you work through the words backwards! In other words, this time, ask what the last three letters are and then show **-ish**. (On the dry erase board write **ish** in green). Then ask what letter comes just before the sound of **-ish**. Show the **urpl** and ask your students if they can hear the sound "**urpl**" in the word **purplish** (in number 5). Continue through the words for the day using the same procedure. (See next page).

---

1. Say the word. Use it in a sentence. Repeat the word.
2. Write the ending sound/s (e.g., -ish, -ly, -ment, etc.).
3. Write the ending base sound (e.g., -eak of freak, ickl of tickl[e], etc.)
4. Write the beginning sounds in front of the base sound to make the word.
5. Have the students check their spelling and if necessary correct their own misspelling.
6. Go to the next word.

---

5. **blackish** Who would buy a **blackish**-blue paint? **blackish**

6. **whitish** Would you want to buy a **whitish** strawberry? **whitish**

7. **Swedish** Do Swedes in Sweden really love **Swedish** meatballs? **Swedish**

8. **Turkish** Do Turks in Turkey take **Turkish** baths? **Turkish**

9. **English** Mr. Engles is learning to speak **English**. **English**

10. ** **Polish** Poles living in Poland ought to be able to speak **Polish**. **Polish**

11. * **parish** In Louisiana what others call a county, they call a **parish**. **parish**

12. * **perish** Perish the thought! Perishable foods can spoil or **perish**. **perish**

13. **childish** I hate to see adults being **childish**. **childish**

14. **selfish** I also hate to see adults being **selfish**. **selfish**

15. **unselfish** Mother Theresa was certainly **unselfish**. **unselfish**

16. **foolish** I hate to see adults being **foolish**. **foolish**

17. **stylish** A model has to know what is **stylish** and what isn't. **stylish**

18. **devilish** My uncle always had a little **devilish** gleam in his eye. **devilish**

19. **impish** He also had an **impish** smile. **impish**

20. **feverish** If you feel **feverish**, you're liable to be sick. **feverish**

21. **snobbish** I really hate people who are **snobbish**. **snobbish**

22. * **finish** I expect to **finish** this test in two more minutes. **finish**

23. **relish** Do you want some **relish** on your hamburger? **relish**

24. **accomplish** What do you expect to **accomplish** this year? **accomplish**

25. **famish** What does **famish** mean? Is it related to **famine**? **famish**

Now tell your students that if they have made all their corrections they will receive an A on their paper. You should be able to quickly do this.

If one of your little Alfred E. Neumanns wrote *finnish* or *Finish* for *finish* and failed to catch his mistake and correct it, you should *NOT* give him an A. Obviously you really shouldn't give him an *E*. So don't give him anything except encouragement that tomorrow he will have a chance to do better and get an *A*. But make sure that he corrects his misspelling. Don't just put a check mark. Have him erase *finnish* or *Finish* and spell *finish* correctly.

Second Day

Have your students take out their AVKO Student Response Book for Sequential Spelling or their special spelling papers.

Today, the first word is **freakishly**. *The clown was acting quite* **freakishly**. **freakishly**

2. **outlandish** His behavior was absolutely **outlandish**. **outlandish**

3. **blemish** The car's paint job had a slight **blemish**. **blemish**

4. **radish** You should have had at least one **radish** in your salad. **radish**

5. **publish** It isn't easy to **publish** a book. **publish**

6. * **polish** You really ought to **polish** your shoes. **polish**

7. **Sweden** Have you ever been to **Sweden**? **Sweden**

8. **Turkey** I haven't been to **Turkey**, either. **Turkey**

9. **Englishman** An **Englishman** ought to speak good English. **Englishman**

10. **Poland** I know some Americans who were born in **Poland**. **Poland**

11. **parishes** In Louisiana, counties are called **parishes**. **parishes**

12. **perishes** Butter **perishes** if it isn't kept refrigerated. **perishes**

13. **childishly** I wish they would stop acting **childishly**. **childishly**

14. **selfishly** I wish they would stop behaving **selfishly**. **selfishly**

15. **unselfishly** They very **unselfishly** donated their time. **unselfishly**

16. **foolishly** They very **foolishly** listened to me. **foolishly**

17. **stylishly** The model was dressed very **stylishly**. **stylishly**

18. **devilishly** My uncle smiled very **devilishly** as he agreed. **devilishly**

19. **impishly** My uncle grinned very **impishly** as he disagreed. **impishly**

20. **solder** Why don't we spell **solder** ("SAH dur") with two **d's**? **solder**

21. **snobbishly** They very **snobbishly** refused our assistance. **snobbishly**

22. **finishes** When Jack **finishes** his homework, tell him to call Jill. **finishes**

23. **relishes** How many kinds of **relishes** can you name? **relishes**

24. **accomplishes** If he **accomplishes** his objective, it will be a miracle. **accomplishes**

25. **famished** I'm **famished** and there isn't any famine. **famished**

* The word *polish* is always pronounced "PAH lish." *Polish* (with a capital P) is a heteronym, two different words with two different pronunciations as in: *Polish* ("PAH'lish") *up on your Polish* ("POH lish") *before you go to Poland.*

The Third Day

On this, the third day, you will begin the slow process of programming your students'God-given computer brains to form the ending –ished correctly. There is no need at this time to encumber a student's mind with rules about the sound of -ed being /t/, as in *wished* ("wish't"), /d/ as in *timed* ("TYH'm-d"), or /id/ as in *added* ("AD id"). All we want to do is to have the students form the habit of spelling /ISH't/ -*ished*. This way, when the rules for adding -ed are presented in their regular language arts books, the students will find it easier to understand them. But, for now, please do not go into any lectures about phonemes and graphemes. It's not at all necessary. In fact, it generally tends to confuse students. However, if some precocious student asks about the rules, tell him that you will discuss the rules with him privately—and keep your word. You can start by saying:

1. **freaky** The weather in April can be very **freaky**. **freaky**

2. **outlandishly** The actress behaved very **outlandishly**. **outlandishly**

3. **blemishes** She had several skin **blemishes**. **blemishes**

4. **radishes**I love to have **radishes** in my salad. **radishes**

5. **publisher** Writing a book is one thing. Finding a **publisher** is another. **publisher**

6. **polishes** A good maid **polishes** the silverware. **polishes**

7. **Irish** The **Irish** know what persecution is. **Irish**

8. **Jewish** My mother's mother was **Jewish**. **Jewish**

9. **Englishmen** Why do **Englishmen** take tea so seriously? **Englishmen**

10. **outlandish** What is so **outlandish** about that? **outlandish**

11. **perishable** You should keep **perishable** food refrigerated. **perishable**

12. **perished**Too many people have **perished** in accidents. **perished**

13. **childishness** I intensely dislike **childishness** in adults. **childishness**

14. **selfishness** I dislike seeing such **selfishness** as well. **selfishness**

15. **unselfishness** I consider **unselfishness** to be a virtue. **unselfishness**

16. **foolishness** I don't pay attention to such **foolishness. foolishness**

17. **stylishness** Who cares about **stylishness**? **stylishness**

18. * **deviltry** Why can't there be "angeltry" as well as **deviltry**? (sic) **deviltry**

19. **squeamish** Nurses shouldn't be **squeamish. squeamish**

20. **solders**An electrician often **solders** connections. **solders**

21. **tongue** A shoe has both eyes and a **tongue. tongue**

22. **finished** We will soon be **finished** with this. **finished**

23. **relished** We **relished** being seated first. **relished**

24. **accomplished** I think we have **accomplished** quite a bit. **accomplished**

25. **famine** There is always a **famine** somewhere in the world. **famine**

* This word is homophonic: devil tree / deviltry Examples: In the Garden of Eden there was deviltry as well as the famous "Devil Tree." There might have been an "Angel Tree" in the Garden of Eden, but I'm sure I've never encountered "angeltry."

The Fourth Day

The fourth day we begin by having the students take out their *AVKO Student Response Book for Sequential Spelling* and open it to page 9 or by having them take out their special spelling sheet.

1. **fiendish** I hate to see someone wearing a **fiendish** grin. **fiendish**

2. **rubbish** Good riddance to bad **rubbish**, I say.**rubbish**

3. **Spanish** I'm glad I know how to speak **Spanish**. **Spanish**

4. **Danish** I can't speak **Danish**, but I sure can eat one. **Danish**

5. **British** The **British** have their own version of English. **British**

6. **polishing** It can be a chore **polishing** silver. **polishing**

7. **Irishmen** There are more **Irishmen** in the U.S. than in Ireland. **Irishmen**

8. **sheepish** She has a **sheepish** smile every time she tells a fib. **sheepish**

9. **brackish** The water tasted awfully **brackish**. **brackish**

10. **outlandishly** The speaker's remarks were **outlandishly** funny. **outlandishly**

11. **perishables** All the **perishables** were placed in a refrigerator. **perishables**

12. **perishing** Even today, thousands are **perishing** from hunger. **perishing**

13. **students** Every child should be able to spell **students**. **students**

14. **Finland** Can you find **Finland** on a globe? **Finland**

15. **Finns** A lot of **Finns** live in Michigan's Upper Peninsula. **Finns**

16. * **Finnish** My buddy Buck speaks **Finnish**. **Finnish**

17. **fetish** The poet Pushkin had a strange foot **fetish**. **fetish**

18. **their** We went over to their house for dinner. **their**

19. **there** While we were there, we had dessert. **there**

20. **soldered** Jack **soldered** the two wires together. **soldered**

21. **tongues** Have you ever heard anyone speaking in **tongues**? **tongues**

22. * **finish** Do you think we'll ever **finish** this test? **finish**

23. **relishing** If you're **relishing** this, you'll like anything. **relishing**

24. **accomplishments** You should list your **accomplishments**. **accomplishments**

25. **unfinished** Do you have any **unfinished** business? **unfinished** **Before** showing this, check your students' papers to see if they have learned to spell the word *unfinished*. Almost every student should have spelled **unfinished** correctly. Now, compare this spelling to the misspellings you collected on the first day. Tell your students you are proud of them. Tell them that they have learned a difficult word without ever having studied the word. Tell them that just by paying attention in class and correcting their mistakes they are learning and learning a great deal.

10

The Fifth Day

1. **nourish** Good parents **nourish** their students. **nourish**

2. **skirmish** The news reported a border **skirmish**. **skirmish**

3. **banish** I wish we could **banish** evil from the earth. **banish**

4. **vanish** I know that when magicians **vanish** it's not magic. **vanish**

5. **diminish** To **diminish** is to make smaller--diminutive even. **diminish**

6. **astonish** Being right shouldn't **astonish** you. **astonish**

7. **punish** You don't have to **punish** yourself. I'll do it for you. **punish**

8. **flourish** When you give students love they should **flourish**. **flourish**

9. **anguish** The u as the w- sound shouldn't cause you any **anguish**. **anguish**

10. **languish** Don't just **languish** in sorrow. Get up and get going. **languish**

11. **vanquish** The Romans failed to **vanquish** the Scots. **vanquish**

12. **lavish** Some parents are too **lavish** in giving presents. **lavish**

13. **abolish** St. Patrick was the first man to try to **abolish** slavery. **abolish**

14. **replenish** We need to **replenish** our supply of fresh water. **replenish**

15. **admonish** Sometimes we have to **admonish** those we love. **admonish**

16. **distinguish** Sometimes it's difficult to **distinguish** tastes. **distinguish**

17. **extinguish** Be sure you completely **extinguish** a camp fire. **extinguish**

18. **relinquish** It's hard for a dictator to **relinquish** control. **relinquish**

10. **establish** You should try to **establish** a good reputation. **establish**

20. **reestablish** It's very hard to **reestablish** a lost reputation. **reestablish**

21. **embellish** You don't have to **embellish** your record. **embellish**

22. **cabin** Was Lincoln really born in a log **cabin**? **cabin**

23. * **robin** The **robin** is the state bird of Michigan. **robin**

24. **griffin** I'll bet you don't know what a **griffin** is. **griffin**

25. * **coffin** Keep **coughin'** and you'll end up in a **coffin**. **coffin**

Homophones: robin / robbin' Robin Hood went around robbin' the rich.
coffin / coughin' I wouldn't want to hear coughin' coming from a coffin.

The Sixth Day

1. **nourishes** It isn't only food that **nourishes** students. **nourishes**

2. **skirmishes** Several soldiers died in the border **skirmishes**. **skirmishes**

3. **banishes** If she **banishes** you from the library for talking, don't come to me for help. **banishes**

4. **vanishes** When a magician **vanishes** on stage it's not really magic. **vanishes**

5. **diminishes** The light outside **diminishes** as evening comes. **diminishes**

6. **astonishes** The power of prayer **astonishes** almost everyone. **astonishes**

7. **punishes** The law **punishes** lawbreakers. **punishes**

8. **flourishes** A child **flourishes** when surrounded by loving care. **flourishes**

9. **anguishes** A parent often anguishes over a sick child. **anguishes**

10. **languishes** Sloth **languishes** in depression. **languishes**

11. **vanquishes** Eventually good **vanquishes** evil. **vanquishes**

12. **lavishes** A millionaire often **lavishes** money on friends. **lavishes**

13. **abolishes** Mr. Jones hopes congress **abolishes** income taxes. **abolishes**

14. **replenishes** Every time he **replenishes** his supply, so do we. **replenishes**

15. **admonishes** Rev. Jim Smith **admonishes** us to be more forgiving. **admonishes**

16. **distinguishes** What **distinguishes** him from others is his mercy. **distinguishes**

17. **extinguishes** When Jim **extinguishes** a flame, it goes out. **extinguishes**

18. **relinquishes** If Tom **relinquishes** his title, I'll be surprised. **relinquishes**

19. **establishes** Rev. Thomas Walton **establishes** new ministries. **establishes**

20. **reestablishes** Albert **reestablishes** friendships. **reestablishes**

21. **embellishes** Thomas **embellishes** all his stories. **embellishes**

22. **cabins** Many great people lived in log **cabins**. **cabins**

23. **robins** Robins are signs of spring in Michigan. **robins**

24. **griffins** I wonder why I've never seen any **griffins**. **griffins**

25. **coffins** Coffins used to be made out of wooden planks. **coffins**

The Seventh Day

1. **nourishing** Milk is highly **nourishing**. **nourishing**

2. **skirmished** The varsity **skirmished** the junior varsity team. **skirmished**

3. **banishes** Our coach **banishes** visitors from our practices. **banishes**

4. **vanishes** After supper, Janet always **vanishes**. **vanishes**

5. **diminishes** My faith in her **diminishes** a little each time she lies. **diminishes**

6. **astonishes** It **astonishes** my dad every time she does dishes. **astonishes**

7. **punishes** John's dad **punishes** him by grounding him. **punishes**

8. **flourishes** An African violet **flourishes** in warm sunlight. **flourishes**

9. **anguishes** My sister **anguishes** over the littlest things. **anguishes**

10. **languishes** When she pouts, she **languishes** in her room. **languishes**

11. **vanquishes** Faith **vanquishes** fear. **vanquishes**

12. **lavishes** A teacher often **lavishes** students with praise. **lavishes**

13. **abolishes** It'll be the day when she **abolishes** homework. **abolishes**

14. **replenishes** Dad **replenishes** the smoke detectors yearly. **replenishes**

15. **admonishes** He **admonishes** us to remind him. **admonishes**

16. **distinguishes** A brave soldier **distinguishes** himself in battle. **distinguishes**

17. **extinguishes** Jack **extinguishes** the campfires correctly. **extinguishes**

18. **relinquishes** It'll be the day when a king **relinquishes** power. **relinquishes**

19. **establishes** A rich man **establishes** credit easily. **establishes**

20. **reestablishes** A wise man **reestablishes** his credit. **reestablishes**

21. **embellishes** A liar often **embellishes** the truth. **embellishes**

22. **cabins** Log **cabins** were once very common. **cabins**

23. **robins** Robins are welcome signs of spring in Ohio. **robins**

24. **griffins** Have you ever seen pictures of **griffins**? **griffins**

25. **coffins** Coffins were once made simply out of wood. **coffins**

After the Seventh Day

Every single day there is a twenty-five-word spelling test. Some days the tests are easier than others, but please don't panic on days like the 16th day when the word *obstetrician* is presented.

REMEMBER: AVKO is *not* concerned about teaching the spelling of any one word *per se*. AVKO *is* concerned with the teaching of basic sounds for both spelling and reading. In the case of words like *obstetrician, physician,* and *electrician,* what is important is the teaching of the -*ician* ending, the roots, and the structural endings, as well as the initial consonant sounds, consonant blends, prefixes, etc.

REMEMBER: Please *speed* your students through the tests. Give the word. Put it in a sentence. Say the word. Spell the word. Have the students (if you can) trace the corrected spelling as they spell it aloud in group chorus. Go on to the next— but make sure your students make an attempt at the spelling *before* you give the correct spelling. **Copying** your spelling does **not** help them learn. **Correcting** their own misspelling **does**.

REMEMBER: Encourage your students to *speed* through these tests. Give the word. Put it in a sentence. Say the word. Spell the word. Have the students (if you can) trace the corrected spelling as they spell it aloud in group chorus. Go on to the next —but make sure your students make an attempt at the spelling *before* you give the correct spelling. *Copying* your spelling does *not* help them learn. *Correcting* their own misspelling **does**.

Immediate Feedback

The most common mistake made in administering the *AVKO Sequential Spelling Tests* is to give the entire test and then correct. This method just *won't* work.

● Give each word separately.

● Say the word. Give it in a sentence.

● Let the students attempt the spelling.

● Give the correct spelling. Let students correct their mistakes.

● Then give the next word. Repeat the process of immediate student self-correction.

Grading

If you desire to give grades for spelling, I would recommend that you give tests for grading purposes separately. You may then grade your students on their learning of the spelling of the sounds—not the words. Sequential Spelling gives permission for parents (and teachers) to duplicate (for their students only) the tests that come after the 40th, 80th, 120th, 160th and 180th days. Read the sentences to your students. All they have to do is fill in the blanks. Notice that you are not testing on the whole word. You are testing only on the spelling patterns taught. (That is why the initial consonants or blends are given to the student.) NOTE: You can use these as a pre-tests, as well as post-tests, to show progress. How you grade these tests is up to you. I recommend that 0-2 wrong = A, 3-4 = B, 5-6 = C, and 7-8 = D.

If your students get more than 8 wrong, I recommend going back over the process to help them learn what they are missing.

Questions most frequently asked concerning Sequential Spelling

1. What are those asterisks (*) and exclamation marks doing next to some words?

The asterisks merely serve as a reminder to the parent/teacher that the word so marked has a **homophone** (same pronunciation, different spelling), has a **heteronym** (same spelling, different word and different pronunciation), or does not follow the normal pattern. For example, *gyp* ** should logically be spelled "*jip.*" But instead of *j* we use the letter "*g.*" Instead of *i* the letter *y* is used. Likewise, the word *proper* ** should logically be spelled "*propper*" just like *hopper*, and *copper*, and *stopper*, but it isn't.

2. Why don't the words used follow grade levels? For example, _unofficially_ is an _11th_ grade word in many schools' regular spelling texts.

Regular spelling texts, as a general rule, pick grade levels for words according to when the words first begin to occur in the curriculum. This would seem to make sense, but it does bring about some rather odd sequences. Since the word *ice* may not occur in the curriculum until the fourth grade (when it appears in the science class), its introduction is delayed until that time even though *nice* may occur in the first grade, *twice* in the second grade, *price* in the fifth, and *rice* in the sixth.

We believe in teaching the phonics necessary for decoding through the back door of spelling and without preaching rules that may or may not be useful. We teach the word *nephew* only after the –ew "yoo" sound has been taught in 12 different words. Notice that the word nephew directly after the homophones **few** and **phew**!

3. Why do you have so many words that are outside the vocabulary of normal adults, such as the word "lyre"?

We don't believe it hurts anyone to learn a new word—but that is not why we use it. We use the word *lyre* as an added practice in sounding out spellings of words having the initial /l/ sound and practice in spelling the ending -*yre*. It also gives the student a pleasant surprise and ego boost when he discovers he can spell a word that he believes he has never heard nor seen before—just because he knows how to spell the sounds.

4. Should I count off for sloppy handwriting?

Since the students get to correct their own spelling, they should be expected to write clearly and legibly. In fact, I recommend that these sequential spelling tests be used for handwriting practice because the patterns, being repetitive, can be a help in developing legible handwriting. I further recommend that if your students print, that they use D'Nealian® manuscript. If your students write, we strongly recommend D'Nealian® cursive. Another excellent system is the Italic by Getty-Dubay. But whatever system you use, we believe that **writing must be legible**. So, yes, by all means, take off for sloppy handwriting (provided the student has no physical disability and has sufficient small motor skills to write legibly).

5. Do I have to use all the words that are in the tests? Can I drop some? Can I change some?

No, you don't have to use them all. You can drop some. You know your students better than I do. Yes, you can substitute other words for the ones I have selected. *The Patterns of English Spelling* is your best reference to select from. If, for example, you would rather start with the -at, bat, rat, cat, sat family, be my guest. You can use your pencil to write in your choices. Every student is different. Don't be afraid to trust your own judgment.

6. Can I give the same test more than once during the day?

Yes. If your students can profit from that, fine. I recommend, however, that you allow a minimum of two hours to pass between re-tests. I also recommend four as the absolute maximum number of times that Sequential Spelling be given in one day, whether repeats or new lessons.

7. I have a child who is a 5th grader. May I use Sequential Spelling 1 to

start one hour, Sequential Spelling 2 to start the 2nd hour, 3 for the third, etc.? I want my child to become as good a reader and speller as possible.

Why not? If it works, it works. If it doesn't, then try something else. You could try going through four days of Sequential Spelling I every day until it is finished and then move through four days of Sequential Spelling II every day, and continue on through four levels of Sequential Spelling in one year.

8. Why are some words in bold print?

The words in **bold print** are those that are the most commonly used words and the most important to learn. You will also notice that some words (like the word **doesn't**) that don't follow regular patterns are repeated many times throughout the series. If your students learn to spell any of the words that are not in bold face, that is a bonus. What I want the students to learn is to spell the most common words and to learn the most common patterns that occur in words. You will discover that most of these patterns consist of only two, three, or four letters. A big word like *misunderstandings* can be broken into the following patterns: *mis/un/der/st/and/ing/s*.

9. Do I have to teach all the homophones and homographs listed?

Absolutely not. I have listed them for your convenience. If you wish to teach them, fine. If you don't, fine. I only ask that when they come up that you definitely use the word in a sentence that helps the student pick the right word. For example: Don't just say **billed**. The students may think about the word **build**. Instead, say something like: "**billed**. *We were* **billed** *for extra carpeting.* **billed**.*"*

10. What does TPES stand for at the bottom of the pages?

TPES stands for *The Patterns of English Spelling*. This book contains all the words that share a common spelling pattern placed on the same page (or pages in the case of families like the -tion family). In our Sequential Spelling Series, I list most of the words in each family, but not all. If a parent/teacher wants to include more or wants to give special assignments to the gifted students, I have included the page references. This book may be purchased from the AVKO Educational Research Foundation, 3084 W. Willard Rd., Clio, MI 48420. For more information call toll free: 1-866-AVKO 612.

11. Can I use the words in Sequential Spelling for composition?

Yes, of course. Having your students create sentences out of the words is good exercise for their minds and will allow you to determine if they truly understand what the words really mean. You may also have them write the entire sentence that you dictate. That will help you help them handle the problems created by speech patterns, such as the "wanna" instead of "want to" and the "whacha gonna" for "what are you going to," etc. As the parent/teacher, you know your students and how many sentences they can handle as homework. You might even want to set time limits such as: Write as many sentences using today's spelling words as you can in 10 minutes.

12. Is there anything I can use to help my students' reading that will also reinforce the spelling?

AVKO's *New Word Families in Sentence Context* may be used in conjunction with Sequential Spelling. The page number given for *The Patterns of English Spelling* (TPES) also works for the *Word Families in Sentence Context*. This book may also be obtained from the AVKO Educational Research Foundation.

For answers to your questions, call: 1-866-AVKO-612 or E-mail info@avko.org

	1st day	2nd day	3rd day	4th day
1.	freakish	freakishly	freaky	fiendish
2.	ticklish	outlandish	outlandishly	**rubbish**
3.	bluish	blemish	blemishes	**Spanish**
4.	purplish	radish	radishes	**Danish**
5.	blackish	publish	publisher	**British**
6.	whitish	** polish	**polishes**	polishing
7.	Swedish	Sweden	**Irish**	two Irishmen
8.	Turkish	Turkey	**Jewish**	sheepish
9.	**English**	Englishman	Englishmen	brackish
10.	** Polish	Poland	outlandish	outlandishly
11.	* parish	parishes	perishable	perishables
12.	* perish	perishes	perished	perishing
13.	childish	childishly	childishness	**students**
14.	**selfish**	selfishly	selfishness	Finland
15.	unselfish	unselfishly	unselfishness	Finns
16.	**foolish**	foolishly	foolishness	* Finnish
17.	stylish	stylishly	stylishness	fetish
18.	devilish	devilishly	deviltry	**their** house
19.	impish	impishly	squeamish	**It's** over **there**.
20.	feverish	! solder	**solders**	**soldered**
21.	snobbish	snobbishly	! tongue	tongues
22.	**finish**	finishes	finished	finishing
23.	**relish**	relishes	relished	relishing
24.	**accomplish**	accomplishes	accomplished	accomplishments
25.	famish	famished	famine	unfinished

* Homophones: parish/perish   A county in Louisiana is called a parish as is a church's congregation. To perish is to die or be destroyed.

** Heteronyms: Polish ("POH lish")/polish ("PAH lish"). The Polish people really know how to polish their shoes.

! Insane words: solder ("SAH dur"). The letter l should really be a d, but it isn't. We must pronounce the word as if it were spelled "sodder." Knowing the word solder becomes a real help in spelling the more common word soldier. The word tongue "TUNG" should be spelled "tung," but it isn't.

	5th day	6th day	7th day	8th day
1.	nourish	nourishes	nourishing	nourishment
2.	skirmish	skirmishes	skirmished	skirmishing
3.	banish	banishes	banished	banishing
4.	**vanish**	vanishes	vanished	vanishing
5.	diminish	diminishes	diminished	diminishing
6.	astonish	astonishes	astonished	astonishment
7.	**punish**	**punishes**	**punished**	**punishment**
8.	flourish	flourishes	flourished	flourishing
9.	anguish	anguishes	anguished	anguishing
10.	languish	languishes	languished	languishing
11.	vanquish	vanquishes	vanquished	vanquishing
12.	lavish	lavishes	lavished	lavishly
13.	abolish	abolishes	abolished	abolition
14.	replenish	replenishes	replenished	plentiful
15.	admonish	admonishes	admonished	admonishing
16.	distinguish	distinguishes	distinguished	distinguishing
17.	extinguish	extinguishes	extinguished	extinguisher
18.	relinquish	relinquishes	relinquished	relinquishing
19.	**establish**	**establishes**	**established**	**establishment**
20.	reestablish	reestablishes	reestablished	reestablishing
21.	embellish	embellishes	embellished	embellishment
22.	**cabin**	cabins	cabinet	cabinetry
23.	***robin**	robins	paraffin	elfin
24.	griffin	griffins	muffin	**muffins**
25.	***coffin**	coffins	ragamuffin	ragamuffins

* Homophones:
robin/robbin' What do you call a red-breasted bird that steals? A robbin' robin.
coffin/coughin' What do you call a casket with a cold? A coughin' coffin.

	9th day	10th day	11th day	12th day
1.	noggin	Mike Goggins	penguin	penguins
2.	origin	origins	original	originally
3.	margin	margins	marginal	marginally
4.	urchin	urchins	toxin	toxins
5.	dolphin	dolphins	intoxicate	intoxication
6.	napkin	napkins	insulin	penicillin
7.	bumpkin	bumpkins	Martin	Martin's friends
8.	pumpkin	pumpkins	gelatin	**! soldering** gun
9.	doeskin	doeskins	hairpin	hairpins
10.	pigskin	pigskins	Austin	Austin's police
11.	goblin	goblins	sequin	sequins
12.	Franklin	Franklin's kite	Cousin Mary	my cousin's car
13.	violin	violins	**! soldier**	**! soldiers**
14.	Berlin	Irving Berlin's songs	solid	solidly
15.	Merlin	Merlin's magic	tongue	tongues
16.	vitamin	vitamins	vital	vitality
17.	basin	basins	second	seconds
18.	moccasin	moccasins	moccasin	moccasins
19.	* **raisin**	raisins	**There's** nothing.	**Their** cat died.
20.	assassin	assassins	assassination	assassinations
21.	assassinate	assassinates	assassinated	assassinating
22.	* **cousin**	cousins	my cousin's car	**They're** not home.
23.	Latin	pectin	That's **theirs**.	We were **there**.
24.	satin	satins	**They're** coming.	We **used to** go **there**.
25.	bulletin	bulletins	**It's too** bad.	**You're supposed to** go.

* Homophones: The following will be repeated and repeated throughout the year: there/their/they're we're/were you're/your/yore

raisin/raisin'/razin'   Even a California Raisin can't go raisin' cane or razin' buildings.

! Insane words:

soldier ("SOH'l jur")   A sol<u>die</u>r may <u>die</u> in battle.
solder ("SAH dur")   We use solder to fasten wires together.
solid ("SAH lid")   The opposite of hollow is solid.
solider ("SAH lid ur")   If a <u>lid</u> is more sol<u>id</u> than its container, it would be sol<u>ider</u>.
tongue ("Tung")   Stick out your tongue and say "ah."

	13th day	**14th day**	**15th day**	**16th day**
1.	**husband**	husbands	Poland	Poland's
2.	brigand	brigands	Roland	Roland's
3.	midland	midlands	garland	garlands
4.	Midland	Midland's	**! island**	**islands**
5.	Newfoundland	Newfoundland's	**! * isle**	**isles**
6.	woodland	woodlands	**! * aisle**	**aisles**
7.	Iceland	Iceland's	Shetland	Portland
8.	Ireland	Ireland's	Maryland	Maryland's
9.	England	England's	errand	errands
10.	Holland	Holland's	thousand	thousands
11.	Greenland	Greenland's	industry	industries
12.	**legend**	legends	legendary	industrial
13.	stipend	stipends	reverence	industrialist
14.	reverend	reverends	Reverend Brown	Rev. Brown
15.	**thing**	**things**	infantry	gallantry
16.	anything	**something**	**nothing**	**everything**
17.	starling	starlings	duckling	ducklings
18.	yearling	yearlings	fledgling	fledglings
19.	poetry	paltry	forestry	geometry
20.	sultry	enter	Elmer Gantry	gantries
21.	pantry	entry	sentry	**country**
22.	pantries	entries	sentries	**countries**
23.	gantry	entrance	carpentry	My **country's** flag
24.	Elmer Gantry	gentry	**winter**	register
25.	gantries	bigotry	wintry	registry

* Homophones:

isle/I'll/aisle   I'll walk down the aisle on the isle of Capri.

! Insane words: isle ("YH'l"); island ("YH lund"); aisle; nothing ("NUH thing")

Notes: Notice how the letter E drops when words such as *enter* and *winter* change to *entry* and *wintry*, respectively. Notice that the -try and -tries endings sound exactly like tree and trees!

	17th day	18th day	19th day	20th day
1.	daub	daubs	daubed	daubing
2.	dauber	daubers	bauble	baubles
3.	**fraud**	frauds	fraudulent	**applause**
4.	defraud	defrauds	defrauded	defrauding
5.	laud	lauds	lauded	lauding
6.	**applaud**	applauds	**applauded**	applauding
7.	maraud	marauds	marauded	marauding
8.	marauder	marauders	Aunt Maud	Auntie Maude
9.	pedlar	pedlars	peddler	peddlers
10.	beggar	beggars	**peculiar**	peculiarity
11.	cedar	cedars	**** friar**	friars
12.	**** liar**	liars	molar	molars
13.	vulgar	pliers	polar	polarity
14.	**hangar**	hangars	solar	**! soldering** gun
15.	**sugar**	sugars	**popular**	**popularity**
16.	burglar	burglars	burglary	burglaries
17.	**similar**	similarly	similarity	similarities
18.	**cellar***	cellars	spectacular	spectacle
19.	pillar	pillars	**particular**	**particularly**
20.	caterpillar	caterpillars	perpendicular	**circle**
21.	**collar**	collars	circular	circularity
22.	scholar	scholars	scholarship	scholarships
23.	cheddar	vinegar	muscular	**muscle**
24.	calendar	calendars	**regular**	regularity
25.	**familiar**	familiarity	irregular	regulations

** Homophones:*

liar/lyre	What do you call a dishonest harp? A liar lyre.
friar/frier/fryer	What do you call a monk that fries chicken? A frier friar or a fryer friar.
cellar/seller	What do you call a basement salesman? A cellar seller.
peddler/pedlar	Peddler is the American spelling. Pedlar is typically British.

! Insane Word: soldering ("SAH'd dur ing")

Note: The letter *u* jumps up and inserts itself between the letters *c* and *l* in words that end *-cle* while the *e* drops with an *-ar* ending. *Particle* becomes *particular*, *circle* becomes *circular*, *muscle* becomes *muscular*, etc.

22

	21st day	22nd day	23rd day	24th day
1.	**angle**	**single**	**triangle**	**rectangle**
2.	**angular**	**singular**	**triangular**	**rectangular**
3.	jugular	lunar	lunacy	lunatic
4.	* **altar**	altars	tartar	mortar
5.	Gibraltar	nectar	bursar	Caesar
6.	**method**	methods	methodical	methodically
7.	**period**	periods	periodical	periodically
8.	medic	medics	**public**	republic
9.	medical	medically	publications	Republican
10.	**medicine**	medicinal	* **symbol**	symbols
11.	**traffic**	garlic	symbolic	symbolism
12.	pacify	pacifies	alcoholic	alcoholism
13.	pacific	Pacific Ocean	stomach	stomach ache
14.	specify	specifies	specified	specifying
15.	specific	specifically	specifications	species
16.	terrify	terrifies	**terrified**	**terrifying**
17.	terrific	terrifically	terror	**It's** over **there.**
18.	science	sciences	**They're** coming.	**There's** a reason.
19.	scientist	scientists	What's ours is **theirs.**	**Their** son won.
20.	scientific	scientifically	unscientific	unscientifically
21.	**magic**	magical	magically	**magician**
22.	**music**	musical	musically	**musician**
23.	**electric**	electrical	electrically	**electrician**
24.	tragic	tragically	**tragedy**	tragedies
25.	strategic	strategically	strategy	strategies

* Homophones:

altar/alter   The minister decided to alter the altar as part of the church alterations.

symbol/cymbal   What do you call a sign for a clashing sound? A cymbal symbol.

Note: The letter *u* jumps up and inserts itself between the letters *g* and *l* in words that end -*gle* while the *e* drops with an -*ar* ending. *Angle* becomes *angular*, *triangle* becomes *triangular*, etc.

	25th day	26th day	27th day	28th day
1.	**picnic**	picnics	**picnicked**	**picnicking**
2.	**panic**	panics	**panicked**	**panicking**
3.	**mimic**	mimics	**mimicked**	**mimicking**
4.	comic	comics	comical	comically
5.	economy	economies	economize	economizing
6.	economic	economical	economically	economist
7.	academy	academies	atomic	dynamite
8.	academic	cosmic	dynamic	dynamo
9.	**clinic**	clinics	clinical	clinically
10.	organic	inorganic	hectic	static
11.	**mechanic**	mechanics	mechanical	mechanically
12.	**! ocean**	citric acid	**drama**	dramas
13.	oceanic	nitric acid	**dramatic**	dramatically
14.	*** scene**	gastric acid	**fanatic**	fanatically
15.	scenic	lyre	**frantic**	frantically
16.	ethnic	lyric	lyrics	lyrical
17.	**hero**	diplomacy	diplomat	diplomatic
18.	heroic	heroically	heroism	diplomatically
19.	**topic**	topical	**Arctic**	Antarctic
20.	tropic	tropics	tropical	Antarctica
21.	**fabric**	fabrics	diabetic	diabetes
22.	*** base**	**basis**	apology	apologies
23.	**basic**	basically	apologetic	**# apologize**
24.	*** centre**	egocentric	obstetrics	obstetrician
25.	centric	eccentric	physics	**physician**

* Homophones:

base/bass	What do you call a real low-down singer? A base bass.
seen/scene	What's a part of a play you just saw? A seen scene.
centre/center	When Americans want to fancy up the name of a center they use the British spelling *centre*.

 # Note: In British English it's –ise instead of –ize. British never apologize, but they do apologise.

! Insane Word: ocean ("OH shun") Note: The letters *ce* form the "sh" digraph and the letters –an are pronounced "un" just as in Ameri*can*, Canadi*an*, tobog*gan*, etc.

24

	29th day	30th day	31st day	32nd day
1.	**surface**	surfaces	surfaced	surfacing
2.	preface	prefaces	prefaced	prefacing
3.	palace	palaces	**necklace**	necklaces
4.	**furnace**	furnaces	terrace	terraces
5.	menace	menaces	menaced	menacing
6.	solace	Wallace	populace	! * Mr. Lovelace
7.	**sauce**	sauces	**saucer**	saucers
8.	saucy	applesauce	saucier	sauciest
9.	* peace	**peaceful**	**peacefully**	peaceable
10.	peacetime	peacemaker	peace officer	peace offering
11.	* **Greece**	Greece's people	Greeks	fleecy
12.	fleece	fleeces	fleeced	fleecing
13.	deuce	deuces	Acey-Deucy	deuce
14.	**office**	offices	**officer**	officers
15.	**service**	**services**	serviced	servicing
16.	disservice	justice	justices	malice
17.	**notice**	notices	noticed	noticing
18.	**practice**	practices	practiced	practicing
19.	apprentice	apprentices	apprenticed	apprenticing
20.	**prejudice**	prejudices	prejudiced	prejudicing
21.	**Alice**	Alice's Restaurant	chalice	chalices
22.	Janice	Janice's place	Venice	Venice's canals
23.	accomplice	accomplices	novice	novices
24.	armistice	armistices	cowardice	injustice
25.	**promise**	**promises**	**promised**	**promising**

* Homophones:

peace/piece   A piece of pie can give peace of mind.
Greece/grease   What do you call Greek oil? Greece grease.

! Insane Word: Lovelace rhymes with necklace. The *lace* is pronounced "*liss*!"

	33rd day	34th day	35th day	36th day
1.	**grocer**	grocers	grocery	groceries
2.	**juice**	juices	juicy	juiciest
3.	sluice	sluices	sluiced	sluicing
4.	**police**	polices	policed	policing
5.	policeman	policemen	policewoman	policewomen
6.	caprice	caprices	Denice	Denice's nephew
7.	Bernice	Bernice's niece	* ! **Nice**, France	Clarice
8.	Felice	Felice's daughter	Denise	Denise's
9.	police work	* **Greece**	valise	valises
10.	* **grease**	greases	greased	greasing
11.	**such**	much too fast	! **anchor**	! * **anchors**
12.	mulch	mulches	mulched	mulching
13.	gulch	gulches	**stomach**	stoma**ch ache**
14.	dry-gulch	dry-gulches	dry-gulched	dry-gulching
15.	**special**	specials	specialty	specialties
16.	# **specialize**	specializes	specialized	specializing
17.	especial	especially	**racial**	racially
18.	**social**	socially	**official**	officials
19.	commercial	commercials	commercially	noncommercial
20.	crucial	crucially	facial	facials
21.	artificial	artificially	unofficial	unofficially
22.	beneficial	beneficially	judicial	sacrificial
23.	antisocial	provincial	judicious	* **They're** going.
24.	glacier	glaciers	prejudicial	**island**
25.	suspicion	suspicions	suspicious	suspiciously

* Homophones:

Greece/grease	What's Greek oil? Greece grease.
Nice/niece	What do you call my nephew's sister who lives in Nice, France? My Nice niece.
there/their/they're	They're building their house over there.

! Insane Words:

Anchor ("ANG kur"); Nice ("NEE-ss"); island; stomach ("STUM ik")

 # Note: In British English –ize words are spelled –ise. The British specialise and Americans specialize.

26

	37th day	38th day	39th day	40th day
1.	**lock**	*** locks**	locked	locking
2.	unlock	unlocks	unlocked	unlocking
3.	padlock	padlocks	padlocked	lockers
4.	**clock**	clocks	clocked	clocking
5.	nine **o'clock**	blocks	blocked	blocking
6.	flock	flocks	blocker	blockers
7.	cock	cocks	cocked	cocking
8.	peacock	peacocks	cocky	cockiest
9.	**rock**	rocks	rocked	rocking
10.	crock	crocks	rocky	rockiest
11.	**knock**	knocks	knocked	knocking
12.	**sock**	*** socks**	socked	socking
13.	**stock**	stocks	stocked	stocking
14.	mock	mocks	mocked	mocking
15.	smock	smocks	hockey	anchored
16.	hock	hocks	hocked	hocking
17.	*** dock**	*** docks**	docked	docking
18.	frock	frocks	cameo	cameos
19.	defrock	defrocks	defrocked	defrocking
20.	shock	shocks	shocked	shocking
21.	duck	*** ducks**	*** ducked**	ducking
22.	**luck**	lucks	lucky	luckiest
23.	cluck	clucks	clucked	clucking
24.	pluck	plucks	plucked	plucking
25.	**buck**	bucks	bucked	bucking

* Homophones:

locks/lox/loughs/lochs   What would a Scotsman use to lock up a lake? A loch lock.
    What would an Irishman use to lock up a lake? A lough lock.
    What would a deli owner use to lock up his salmon? Lox locks.
socks/sox   Some people wear socks. Others wear sox.
ducked/duct   What the heat run did when shot at. The duct ducked.
pair of doc's/pair of docks/paradox Is a paradox a pair of doc's who own a pair of docks?

Grading

If your particular curriculum requires that a grade be given for spelling, we would recommend that tests for grading purposes be given at a separate time and that the students be graded on their learning of the spelling of the sounds — not the words as the suggested tests for grading purposes are constructed to do. AVKO gives permission for parents to duplicate the tests for their home school only. Read the sentences to your students. All they have to do is fill in the blanks. Notice that you are not testing on the whole word. You are testing only on the spelling patterns taught. That is why the initial consonants or blends are given to the child. Note: You can use this as a pre-test as well as a post-test to show real gains. How you grade these tests is up to you. You could use the 0-1 wrong = A, 2-4 = B, 5-7 = C, 8-10 = D. We don't expect that you'll have any E's.

Evaluation Test #1 (After 40 Days)

	Sentence	Pattern being tested	Lesson word is in
1.	We have some unfin**ished** business to attend to.	ished	4
2.	Every house should have a fire extingu**isher**.	isher	8
3.	Do you like bran muff**ins**?	ins	8
4.	You should try walking in another's moccas**ins**.	ins	12
5.	Would you like an en**try** level job?	try	14
6.	The English brought star**lings** to America.	lings	14
7.	Speakers love appl**ause**.	ause	20
8.	No one likes to be defr**auded**.	auded	19
9.	I wish you wouldn't be so part**icular**.	icular	19
10.	Famili**arity** breeds contempt.	arity	18
11.	Please give at least one spec**ific** example.	ific	21
12.	My older sister is an electri**cian**.	cian	24
13.	My older brother is a musi**cian**.	cian	24
14.	We told him not to panic, but he still panic**ked**.	ked	27
15.	Afterwards, he was very apolog**etic**.	etic	27
16.	Have you not**iced** how quickly you're learning?	iced	31
17.	AVKO spe**cial**izes in helping people learn.	cial	34
18.	It is cru**cial** that you learn certain spelling concepts.	cial	33
19.	It will prove benefi**cial** if you can master them.	cial	33
20.	Careful watching of commer**cials** can help your reading.	cial	34

* These words were never given, but other forms of these words were used.

Name_____   **Date**_____

TEST #1

Please, please, please do NOT start until your teacher gives you the directions.
You must stay with your teacher as she reads the sentences.
All you have to do is to fill in the blanks with the missing letters.

1. We have some unfin_____ business to attend to.

2. Every house should have a fire extingu_____.

3. Do you like bran muff_____?

4. You should try walking in another's moccas_____.

5. Would you like an en_____ level job?

6. The English brought star_____ to America.

7. Speakers love appl_____.

8. No one likes to be defr_____.

9. I wish you wouldn't be so part_____.

10. Famili_____ breeds contempt.

11. Please give at least one spec_____ example.

12. My older sister is an electri_____.

13. My older brother is a musi_____.

14. We told him not to panic, but he still panic_____.

15. Afterwards, he was very apolog_____.

16. Have you not_____ how quickly you're learning?

17. AVKO spe_____izes in helping people learn.

18. It is cru_____ that you learn certain spelling concepts.

19. It will prove benefi_____ if you can master them.

20. Careful watching of commer_____ can help your reading.

	41st day	42nd day	43rd day	44th day
1.	muck	mucks	mucked	mucking
2.	puck	pucks	Anchorage, AK	**headache**
3.	chuck	chucks	chucked	chucking
4.	woodchuck	woodchucks	Chuck's name	**stuck**
5.	suck	sucks	sucked	sucking
6.	**truck**	trucks	trucked	trucking
7.	**struck**	Huck Finn	trucker	truckers
8.	article	articles	circular	**particular**
9.	**particle**	**particles**	**circus**	**particularly**
10.	**circle**	circles	circled	circling
11.	encircle	encircles	encircled	encircling
12.	**uncle**	uncles	**Uncle** Tim	my **uncle's** house
13.	**icicle**	icicles	**vehicle**	vehicles
14.	**bicycle**	bicycles	**vehicular**	**cameo**
15.	tricycle	tricycles	**biscuit**	**biscuits**
16.	* **muscle**	muscles	**muscular**	muscularity
17.	**miracle**	miracles	**miraculous**	miraculously
18.	**spectacle**	spectacles	**spectacular**	spectacularly
19.	obstacle	obstacles	debacle	debacles
20.	manacle	manacles	manacled	manacling
21.	oracle	oracles	oracular	**islands**
22.	**act**	* **acts**	acted	acting
23.	actor	actors	active	**action**
24.	enact	enacts	enacted	enacting
25.	re-enact	re-enacts	re-enacted	re-enacting

* Homophones:

muscle/mussel	What do you call clam-like strength? Mussel muscle.
acts/ax/axe	What do you call it when a hatchet goes on stage? The ax acts.

	45th day	46th day	47th day	48th day
1.	**fact**	* **facts**	faction	factions
2.	factor	factors	factored	factoring
3.	* **tract**	* **tracts**	tractor	tractors
4.	**attract**	attracts	attracted	attracting
5.	attractor	attractive	**attraction**	attractions
6.	distract	distracts	distracted	distracting
7.	tractor	tractors	distraction	distractions
8.	abstract	abstracts	abstraction	abstracting
9.	extract	extracts	extracted	extraction
10.	detract	detracts	detracting	detraction
11.	retract	retracts	retracted	retraction
12.	**subtract**	subtracts	subtracting	**subtraction**
13.	refract	refracts	refracting	refraction
14.	** __con__tract	__con__tracts	__con__tracted	__con__tracting
15.	** con__tract__	con__tracts__	con__tracted__	con__tracting__
16.	__con__tractor	__con__tractors	con__traction__	con__tractions__
17.	* **pact**	pacts	cataract	cataracts
18.	__com__pact	__com__pacts	com__pactor__	com__pactors__
19.	com**pact**	com**pacts**	com__pacted__	com__pacting__
20.	impact	impacts	impacted	impacting
21.	**exact**	exacts	exacted	exacting
22.	* **tact**	* **tacts**	tactic	tactics
23.	**character**	characters	characteristic	characteristics
24.	connecter	connecters	characteristically	uncharacteristically
25.	**fracture**	fractures	fractured	fracturing

* Homophones:

facts/fax	What is information from a facsimile? Fax facts.
tacts/tax/tacks	A sailing ship tacts. Stores charge tax for tacks.
pact/packed	They signed a peace pact. They packed up their belongings.
tract/tracked	The dogs tracked the fox to a large tract of swamp land.
tact/tacked	They tried a new tact. They tacked up a poster.

** Heteronyms:

contract/contract	You sign a **con**tract. You con**tract** a disease.
compact/compact	To com**pact** is to make small. A **com**pact is small.

	49th day	50th day	51st day	52nd day
1.	**direct**	directs	directed	directing
2.	director	directors	directive	**directions**
3.	erect	erects	erected	erecting
4.	**correct**	corrects	corrected	correcting
5.	incorrect	correctly	corrective	**correction**
6.	** <u>per</u>fect	<u>per</u>fectly	perfective	**perfection**
7.	** per<u>fect</u>	per<u>fect</u>s	perfected	perfecting
8.	infect	infects	infected	**infection**
9.	* **affect**	affects	affecting	**affection**
10.	* **effect**	effects	effective	effectively
11.	**defect**	defects	defective	defection
12.	**dejected**	dejection	reject	**rejection**
13.	inject	injection	**! cello**	cello
14.	** <u>ob</u>ject	<u>ob</u>jects	**objective**	objectively
15.	** ob<u>ject</u>	ob<u>ject</u>s	objected	**objection**
16.	** <u>proj</u>ect	<u>proj</u>ects	projector	**projection**
17.	** pro<u>ject</u>	pro<u>ject</u>s	projected	projecting
18.	** <u>sub</u>ject	<u>sub</u>jects	subjective	subjection
19.	** sub<u>ject</u>	sub<u>ject</u>s	subjected	subjecting
20.	**elect**	elects	elected	electing
21.	elector	electors	elective	**election**
22.	**select**	selects	selected	selecting
23.	selector	selectors	selective	**selection**
24.	intellect	intellects	intelligent	intelligence
25.	**neglect**	neglects	neglected	neglecting

* Homophones: affect/effect   The most **E**ffective way we have found to teach the difference is by using the TH**E** test.   Whenever you can put the word *the* before "uh FEK't" spell it **e**ffect. Otherwise spell it **a**ffect.

** Heteronyms:

object/object	I object ("ub JEK't") to being the object ("AH'b jekt") of ridicule.
perfect/perfect	I want to perfect ("pur FEK't") my technique. Then I'll be perfect.
project/project	I don't project ("proh JEK't") my voice. I finished my project ("PRAH jekt").
subject/subject	Don't subject ("sub JEK't") me to being the subject ("SUB jekt") of an article.

32

	53rd day	54th day	55th day	56th day
1.	reflect	*** reflects**	reflected	reflecting
2.	reflector	reflectors	reflective	reflections
3.	deflect	deflects	deflected	deflection
4.	inflect	inflects	inflective	inflection
5.	genuflect	genuflects	genuflecting	genuflection
6.	**expect**	expects	**expected**	expecting
7.	retrospect	disrespect	**unexpected**	**expectations**
8.	**respect**	respects	respected	respective
9.	**inspect**	inspects	inspected	inspecting
10.	inspector	inspectors	inspection	inspections
11.	prospect	prospects	prospected	prospecting
12.	prospector	prospectors	prospective	suspicious
13.	** **sus**pect	**sus**pects	suspicion	suspicions
14.	** su**spect**	su**spects**	suspected	suspecting
15.	sect	*** sects**	section	dissection
16.	dissect	dissects	dissected	dissecting
17.	bisect	bisects	bisecting	bisection
18.	intersect	intersects	intersected	intersection
19.	architect	architects	architecture	detective
20.	**detect**	detects	detected	detecting
21.	**protect**	protects	protected	protecting
22.	hectic	hectically	protective	**protection**
23.	**electric**	electrical	electrically	electrician
24.	electricity	**insect**	**insects**	imperfect
25.	lecture	lectures	lectured	lecturing

* Homophones: sects/sex

| sex/sects | What do you call exclusively male or female religions? Sex sects. |
| reflex/reflects | What do you call the automatic bounces of light waves? The reflects reflex. |

** Heteronyms:

| suspect/suspect | I suspect ("suh SPEK't") that he knew the suspect ("SUS spek't") personally. |

	57th day	58th day	59th day	60th day
1.	**strict**	strictly	restrictive	restrictions
2.	restrict	restricts	restricted	restricting
3.	constrict	constricts	constricted	constricting
4.	**district**	districts	constrictive	constrictions
5.	** **ad**dict	ad**dict**s	addictive	addiction
6.	** ad**dict**	ad**dict**s	addicted	addicting
7.	**predict**	predicts	predicted	predicting
8.	predictor	predictors	predictive	prediction
9.	edict	edicts	contradiction	contradictions
10.	**contradict**	contradicts	contradicted	contradicting
11.	Benedict	Benedict's	benediction	benedictions
12.	interdict	interdicts	interdicted	interdicting
13.	**! indict**	indicts	indicted	indicting
14.	** **con**vict	**con**victs	conviction	convictions
15.	** con**vict**	con**vict**s	convicted	convicting
16.	evict	evicts	evicted	evicting
17.	afflict	afflicts	afflicted	afflicting
18.	derelict	derelicts	**! cello**	**cello**
19.	depict	depicts	depicted	depicting
20.	***picture**	pictures	pictured	picturing
21.	***pitcher**	pitchers	pitching	pitches
22.	concoct	concocts	concocted	concocting
23.	**doctor**	doctors	doctored	concoction
24.	proctor	proctors	proctored	proctoring
25.	Victor	**Victoria**	**victory**	**victorious**

* Homophones:

pitcher/picture — What do you call a photo of a hurler? A pitcher picture. Note: We know that picture *should* be pronounced "PIK chur" as opposed to pitcher ("PICH ur"). However, enough people mispronounce the word that we list it as a homophone so you can play with them if you desire.

** Heteronyms:

addict/addict — An addict ("AD dik't") should not try to addict ("uh DIK't") someone else.
convict/convict — Yes, you can convict ("kun VIK't") a convict ("KAH'n vik't") of a crime.

! Insane Words: indict ("in DYH't") You would think that indict would be spelled "indight" or "indite" but it isn't. Since the root *dict* helps us understand the meaning, we have never changed the spelling as we did the pronunciation. The word cello is pronounced as if it were "**Ch**ello."

34

	61st day	62nd day	63rd day	64th day
1.	** con**duct**	conducts	conducted	conducting
2.	** **con**duct	conductors	conductive	conduction
3.	deduct	deducts	deducted	deducting
4.	deductive	deductively	deduction	deductions
5.	deduce	deduces	deduced	deducing
6.	induce	induces	induced	inducing
7.	inductive	inductively	induction	inductions
8.	induct	inducts	inducted	inducting
9.	abduct	abducts	abducted	abduction
10.	product	products	productive	production
11.	** pro**duce**	produces	produced	producing
12.	** **pro**duce	viaducts	producer	producers
13.	instruct	instructs	instructed	instructing
14.	instructor	instructors	instructive	instructions
15.	con**struct**	con**structs**	constructed	constructing
16.	**con**struct	**con**structs	constructive	construction
17.	obstruct	obstructs	obstructed	obstruction
18.	* **duct**	* **ducts**	doodler	doodlers
19.	noodle	noodles	poodle	poodles
20.	doodle	doodles	doodled	doodling
21.	* **wood**	woods	wooden	woodenly
22.	* **would**	would	wouldn't	wouldn't
23.	stood	withstood	understood	misunderstood
24.	redwoods	hardwood	plywood	dogwood
25.	good	goods	hard goods	soft goods

* Homophones:

duct/ducked — A heat duct carries hot air from a furnace. The batter ducked a wild pitch.
ducts/ducks/duck's/ducks' — Donald Duck ducks ducts. Will a duck's tear ducts produce tears?
would/wood — What would happen if a woodchuck would chuck wood?

	65th day	66th day	67th day	68th day
1.	**hood**	hoods	hooded	hooding
2.	statehood	**falsehood**	falsehoods	sainthood
3.	**manhood**	**womanhood**	**fatherhood**	**motherhood**
4.	**brotherhood**	**sisterhood**	boyhood	girlhood
5.	**childhood**	**likelihood**	**neighborhood**	neighborhoods
6.	**flood**	floods	flooded	flooding
7.	**blood**	bloody	**! Beethoven**	**! Beethoven**
8.	fluid	fluids	**splendid**	splendidly
9.	valid	validly	validity	pyramid
10.	**** invalid**	invalidly	invalidity	stupidly
11.	Druid	Druids	**stupid**	stupidity
12.	*** rude**	**crude**	prude	prudes
13.	**dude**	dudes	duded	duding
14.	elude	eludes	eluded	eluding
15.	nude	nudes	illusive	**illusion**
16.	elude	eludes	eluded	eluding
17.	**attitude**	attitudes	elusive	elusion
18.	allude	alludes	alluded	allusion
19.	delude	deludes	deluded	**delusion**
20.	intrude	intruders	intrusive	intrusion
21.	protrude	protrudes	protruded	protrusion
22.	extrude	extrudes	extruded	extrusion
23.	include	including	inclusive	inclusion
24.	conclude	concluding	conclusive	**conclusion**
25.	**altitude**	altitudes	multitude	multitudes

* Homophones:
rude/rood/rued   The carpenter rued the day he made an impolite cross, a rude rood.

** Heteronyms:
invalid ("in VAL id")/invalid ("IN vuh lid") Can an invalid be invalid?

! Insane word: Beethoven ("BAY toh vun")

#Tricky Words: altitude / attitude

	69th day	70th day	71st day	72nd day
1.	* climb	climbs	climbed	climbing
2.	limb	limbs	climber	climbers
3.	comb	combs	combed	combing
4.	tomb	tombs	tombstone	tombstones
5.	womb	wombs	* lamb	lambs
6.	thumb	thumbs	thumbed	thumbing
7.	crumb	crumbs	bomber	bombers
8.	* bomb	bombs	bombed	bombing
9.	dumb	dumber	dumbest	dumb
10.	debt	debts	debtor	debtors
11.	* gnat	gnats	leprechaun	leprechauns
12.	gnaw	gnaws	gnawed	gnawing
13.	gnarl	gnarls	gnarled	gnarling
14.	* gnome	gnomes	*gnu	*gnus
15.	* sign	signs	signature	signing
16.	design	designs	designation	designing
17.	* align	aligns	aligned	alignment
18.	malign	maligns	malignant	malignancy
19.	* deign	deigns	deigned	deigning
20.	* reign	reigns	reigned	reigning
21.	foreign	foreigner	foreigners	**They're** all right.
22.	alm	alms	qualms	They won **their** case.
23.	palm	palms	Palmer	palmistry
24.	calm	calms	calmed	calming
25.	psalm	psalms	salmon	salve

* Homophones:

climb/clime	Go climb a tree. Find a better climate or clime. Your choice.
bomb/balm	What do you call an ointment that doesn't work? A balm bomb.
gnat/Nat	Nat swallowed a gnat.
lamb/lam	Mary's lamb was on the lam.
gnu/new/knew	I knew the new gnu would get homesick.
gnus/news	No gnus is bad news for a zoo.
gnome/Nome	What do you call an Alaskan dwarf? A Nome gnome.
sign/sine	Knowing what a sine is is a sign of a mathematician.
align/a line	What do you call making a line parallel? To align a line.
Dane/deign	Will the Dane deign to eat an American Danish?
rain/reign/rein	During Elizabeth's reign they had to rein in Walter when it began to rain.

	73rd day	74th day	75th day	76th day
1.	! answer	answers	answered	answering
2.	! who	who's	! * whose book	They're too fast.
3.	! * sword	swords	swordfish	swordfight
4.	! * wrap	* wraps	* wrapped	wrapping
5.	! * wring	* wrings	* wrung	* wringing
6.	! wreck	* wrecks	wrecked	wrecking
7.	! wrecker	wreckers	wren	wrens
8.	! wrath	wrathful	! * whole	* wholly
9.	! wreath	wreaths	! wrist	wrists
10.	! wren	wrens	! writ	writs
11.	! wrench	wrenches	wrenched	wrenching
12.	! wrestle	wrestles	wrestled	wrestling
13.	! wrestler	wrestlers	! wrong	wrongs
14.	! wrinkle	wrinkles	wrinkled	wrinkling
15.	! write	writes	written	writing
16.	! writer	writers	! salve	It's too easy.
17.	! wright	wrights	wrought	Edmund Cartwright
18.	! writhe	writhes	writhed	writhing
19.	grease	greases	greased	greasing
20.	lease	leases	* leased	leasing
21.	release	releases	released	releasing
22.	cease	ceases	ceased	deceased
23.	crease	creases	creased	creasing
24.	increase	increases	increased	increasing
25.	decrease	decreases	decreased	decreasing

* Homophones:

who's/whose	Who's going to help with whose homework?
rap/wrap	What do you call the end of Hammer's recording session? A rap wrap.
rapped/rapt/wrapped	Hammer rapped. The audience was rapt. We wrapped it up.
ring/wring	You can wring a chicken's neck or put a ring on a finger.
rung/wrung	Jack wrung his hands when he broke a rung on his dad's ladder.
Rex/wrecks	Rex gets into too many wrecks.
whole/hole	What do you call a complete void? A whole hole.
wholly/holy	What do you call completely religious? Wholly holy.
right/write/rite/wright	Bruce Wright should always write a rite right.
Greece/grease	What do you call olive oil? Greece grease.
leased/least	At least he leased a decent car.
sword/soared	What happened when King Arthur threw Excalibur? The sword soared.

! Insane Words: Notice the w is silent in these words.

38

	77th day	78th day	79th day	80th day
1.	**sweat**	sweats	**sweater**	sweating
2.	**threat**	threats	**They're** crazy.	sweaters
3.	**threaten**	threatens	threatened	threatening
4.	* **favor**	favors	favored	favoring
5.	* **favour**	favours	favoured	favouring
6.	* **favorable**	favorably	**favorite**	favorites
7.	* **favourable**	favourably	**favourite**	favourites
8.	* **flavor**	flavors	flavored	flavoring
9.	* **flavour**	flavours	flavoured	flavouring
10.	* **savor**	savors	savored	savoring
11.	* **savour**	savours	savoured	savouring
12.	* **saviour**	saviours	**savior**	saviors
13.	**deaf**	deafen	deafens	deafening
14.	**beef**	beefs	beefed	beefing
15.	beefy	beefier	beefiest	reef
16.	**leave**	leaves	**left**	leaving
17.	cleave	cleaves	cleft/cleaved	cleaving
18.	cleaver	cleavers	weaver	weavers
19.	heave	heaves	heaved	heaving
20.	weave	weaves	weaved	weaving
21.	bereave	bereaves	bereft/bereaved	bereaving
22.	**heavy**	heavier	heaviest	heavily
23.	heavyweight	heavyweights	Their boss left.	He went **there, too.**
24.	**sleeve**	sleeves	They're not there.	**Their** dog went **there.**
25.	re**cei**ve	re**cei**ves	re**cei**ved	re**cei**ving

---

* **Homophones:** The following homophones that end -or are standard American spellings. Those that end -our are standard British spellings.

favor/favour	labor/labour	vigor/vigour	armor/amour
favorable/favourable	neighbor/neighbour	behavior/behaviour	humor/humour
flavor/flavour	harbor/harbour	valor/valour	rumor/rumour
savor/savour	rancor/rancour	color/colour	tumor/turmour
savior/saviour	ardor/ardour	parlor/parlour	honor/honour
	odor/odour	clamor/clamour	vapor/vapour
	rigor/rigour	glamour/glamour	fervor/fervour

Evaluation Test #2

(After 80 Days)

	Pattern being tested	Lesson word is in
1. It would be a mir**acle** if Chicago won the series.	acle	41
2. The patient made a mir**aculous** recovery.	aculous	43
3. The two countries signed a non-aggression p**act**.	act	45
4. Sugar attr**acts** ants.	acts	46
5. Do you like previews of coming attr**actions**?	actions	48
6. We stand corr**ected**.	ected	51
7. Do you need dir**ections** on how to get there?	ections	52
8. You really should wear prot**ective** headgear.	ective	55
9. We attended three l**ectures** last year.	ectures	54
10. That patient is on a restr**icted** diet.	icted	59
11. How many of the psychic's pred**ictions** came true?	ictions	60
12. How many heat d**ucts** are there in this room?	ucts	62
13. My brother works for a constr**uction** company.	uction	64
14. I think my sister has a real attit**ude** problem.	ude	65
15. How do you think I arrived at that concl**usion**?	usion	68
16. What would you like inscribed on your t**omb**stone?	omb	71
17. Have you seen the latest house des**igns**?	igns	70
18. Our national debt seems to keep incr**easing**.	easing	76
19. I don't like to be threat**ened** by anyone.	ened	79
20. We gave them new sw**eaters** for their anniversary.	eaters	80

40

Name_____Date_____

Evaluation Test #2

1. It would be a mir_____ if Chicago won the series.

2. The patient made a mirac_____ recovery.

3. The two countries signed a non-aggression p_____.

4. Sugar attr_____ ants.

5. Do you like previews of coming attr_____?

6. We stand corr_____.

7. Do you need dir_____ on how to get there?

8. You really should wear prot_____ headgear.

9. We attended three l_____ last year.

10. That patient is on a restr_____ diet.

11. How many of the psychic's pred_____ came true?

12. How many heat d_____ are there in this room?

13. My brother works for a constr_____ company.

14. I think my sister has a real attit_____ problem.

15. How do you think I arrived at that concl_____?

16. What would you like inscribed on your t_____ stone?

17. Have you seen the latest house des_____?

18. Our national debt seems to keep incr_____.

19. I don't like to be threat_____ by anyone.

20. We gave them new sw_____ for their anniversary.

41

	81st day	82nd day	83rd day	84th day
1.	**receive**	receives	received	receiving
2.	receiver	receivers	receptive	reception
3.	deceive	deceives	deceived	deceiving
4.	receipt	receipts	deceptive	deception
5.	conceive	conceives	conceived	conceiving
6.	concept	concepts	conceivable	conception
7.	misconceive	misconceives	misconceived	misconceiving
8.	inconceivable	inconceivably	ceiling	misconception
9.	preconceive	preconceives	preconceived	preconception
10.	novel	novels	novelty	novelties
11.	grovel	grovels	groveled grovelled	groveling grovelling
12.	**shovel**	shovels	**shoveled shovelled**	shoveling shovelling
13.	swivel	swivels	swiveled swivelled	swiveling swivelling
14.	shrivel	shrivels	shriveled shrivelled	shriveling shrivelling
15.	snivel	snivels	sniveled snivelled	sniveling snivelling
16.	revel	revels	reveled revelled	reveling revelling
17.	**level**	levels	leveled levelled	leveling levelling
18.	bevel	bevels	beveled bevelled	beveling bevelling
19.	**dreadful**	dreadfully	gleeful	gleefully
20.	spiteful	spitefully	**peaceful**	**peacefully**
21.	**forceful**	forcefully	resourceful	resourcefully
22.	**shameful**	shamefully	**eyeful**	eyefuls
23.	**handful**	handfuls	armful	armfuls
24.	**spoonful**	spoonfuls	**mouthful**	mouthfuls
25.	pocketful	pocketfuls	teaspoonful	teaspoonfuls

*** Note:

All of the -el words on this page may have the -ed or -ing added without doubling the l as shown in American English. British English always doubles the letter l in these situations. AVKO prefers following the British style. However, even an American should be consistent and either always double the -l when adding -ed or -ing to these -el words or never.

	85th day	86th day	87th day	88th day
1.	**helpful**	helpfully	thankful	thankfully
2.	**skillful**	skillfully	harmful	harmfully
3.	**cheerful**	**cheerfully**	powerful	powerfully
4.	**eager**	**eagerly**	eagerness	eagerly
5.	meager	tiger	tigers	meagerly
6.	**cabbage**	cabbages	cribbage	garbage
7.	**courage**	courageous	courageously	encouragement
8.	**encourage**	encourages	encouraged	encouraging
9.	discourage	discourages	discouraged	discouraging
10.	**image**	images	message	messages
11.	**bandage**	bandages	bandaged	bandaging
12.	pilgrimage	orphanage	sausage	sausages
13.	scrimmage	scrimmages	**luggage**	breakage
14.	rummage	vantage	carriage	carriages
15.	mileage	**advantage**	advantages	advantageous
16.	**marriage**	marriages	wreckage	**storage**
17.	**package**	packages	packaged	packaging
18.	**village**	villages	villager	villagers
19.	**damage**	damages	**damaged**	damaging
20.	**manage**	manages	**managed**	**managing**
21.	**manager**	managers	management	passageway
22.	patronage	parsonage	**passage**	passages
23.	**average**	averages	averaged	averaging
24.	percentage	percentages	**shortage**	shortages
25.	hostage	hostages	**language**	languages

Note: Words that have just one syllable in their base ending in -age rhyme with age and page. The -age words on this page have more than one syllable in their base and rhyme with the -idge ("ij") words.

	89th day	90th day	91st day	92nd day
1.	**cottage**	cottages	postage	wattage
2.	beverage	beverages	dosage	homage
3.	ravage	ravages	ravaged	ravaging
4.	**college**	colleges	collegiate	college
5.	**privilege**	privileges	privileged	privilege
6.	sacrilege	sacrileges	sacrilegious	sacrilege
7.	**huge**	hugely	Bridget	Bridget's
8.	**ridge**	ridges	ridged	ridging
9.	**bridge**	bridges	bridged	bridging
10.	cartridge	cartridges	midget	midgets
11.	partridge	partridges	widget	widgets
12.	**fudge**	fudges	fudged	fudging
13.	nudge	nudges	nudged	nudging
14.	smudge	smudges	smudged	smudging
15.	grudge	grudges	grudged	grudging
16.	begrudge	begrudges	begrudged	begrudging
17.	budge	budges	budged	budging
18.	**budget**	budgets	budgeted	budgeting
19.	**straight**	straights**	straighter	straightest
20.	**straighten**	straightens	straightened	straightening
21.	**! laugh**	laughs	laughed	laughing
22.	**! laughter**	taught	daughter	daughters
23.	**caught**	fraught	naught	naughty
24.	**! slaughter**	slaughters	slaughtered	slaughtering
25.	**! daughter**	daughters	my daughter's car	my daughters' cars

! Insane Words: laugh ("laff") and laughter ("LAF tur") and daughter ("DAW tur") and caught ("KAW't") Note: In those few dialects that do not distinguish between the "AW" and "AH" vowels, the words *cot* ("KAH't") and *caught* ("KAW't") are homophones.

44

	93rd day	94th day	95th day	96th day
1.	* weigh	weighs	* weighed	weighing
2.	* weight	weights	weighty	weightiest
3.	* sleigh	sleighs	sleighed	sleighing
4.	* neigh	neighs	neighed	neighing
5.	neighbor	neighbors	neighborhood	neighborhoods
6.	eagle	eagles	bugle	bugles
7.	beagle	beagles	bugler	buglers
8.	Mr. Nagle	Mrs. Nagle's	They're not going.	Their dog died.
9.	finagle	finagles	finagled	finagling
10.	inveigle	inveigles	inveigled	inveigling
11.	bah humbug	breaker	broke	breakers
12.	* break	breaks	broken	breaking
13.	breakfast	breakfasts	freak	freaks
14.	* steak	steaks	squeak	squeaks
15.	* weak	teak	teakwood	squeaking
16.	weaken	weakens	weakened	weakening
17.	beak	beaks	squeaky	squeaked
18.	* peak	peaks	leaky	squeakiest
19.	* leak	leaks	leaked	leaking
20.	speak	speaks	spoke	speaking
21.	speaker	speakers	spoken	streaker
22.	streak	streaks	streaked	streaking
23.	sneak	sneaks	sneaked	sneaking
24.	sneaker	sneakers	sneaky	sneakiest
25.	* creak	creaks	creaked	creaking

* Homophones:

neighbor/neighbour	British English uses –our in all the neighbour words from neighbouring to neighbourhood.
peak/peek/pique	A peek at a mountain peak might pique your curiosity.
weigh/way/whey	By the way, how much does a bowl of curds and whey weigh.
weighed/wade	You can wade in water. They weighed their dog.
weight/wait	Wait for the correct weight.
sleigh/slay	To kill a sled is to slay a sleigh.
neigh/nay	Horses neigh. They voted nay instead of aye.
steak/stake	I love to eat steak. You can pound a stake into the ground.
break/brake	Give me a break. Step on the brake.
weak/week	A poor seven days is a weak week.
creak/creek	Doors creak. I like to fish in a creek.
leak/leek	A leak (such as gas) can be dangerous. A leek can be eaten.

	97th day	98th day	99th day	100th day
1.	shriek	shrieks	shrieked	shrieking
2.	spook	spooks	spooked	spooking
3.	spooky	spookier	spookiest	gadzooks
4.	eke	ekes	eked	eking
5.	duke	dukes	Luke	Luke's
6.	fluke	flukes	juke box	nuclear
7.	nuke	nukes	nuked	nuking
8.	rebuke	rebukes	rebuked	rebuking
9.	*** haul**	hauls	hauled	hauling
10.	**overhaul**	overhauls	overhauled	overhauling
11.	caterwaul	caterwauls	caterwauled	caterwauling
12.	*** Paul**	Paul's	Saul	Saul's
13.	*** caul**	cauls	cauliflower	Pauline
14.	**fault**	**faults**	faulted	faulting
15.	faulty	faultier	faultiest	faulty
16.	excel	excels	excelled	excelling
17.	lapel	lapels	excellent	excellence
18.	**! Michel**	**Michel's****	**their** choice	**They're great**!
19.	to **rebel**	she rebels	rebelled	rebelling
20.	a **rebel**	two rebels	rebellion	rebellious
21.	repel	repels	repelled	repelling
22.	repulse	repulses	repulsed	repulsive
23.	**compel**	compels	compelled	compelling
24.	**hotel**	hotels	compulsive	compulsion
25.	dispel	dispels	dispelled	dispelling

* Homophones:

haul/hall   They had to haul away the garbage from the hall.
caul/call   If you know what a caul is, call me.
Paul/pall   Paul knows what a pall is and has been a pallbearer.

** Heteronyms:
rebel ("re BEL")/rebel ("REB'l") A rebel is one who loves to rebel against authority.

! Insane Word: Michel ("mee SHELL") is a French name. Do not confuse with Michael ("MY k'l"). Michel is masculine. The feminine is Michelle.

46

	101st day	102nd day	103rd day	104th day
1.	propel	propels	propelled	propelling
2.	**motel**	motels	propulsive	jet propulsion
3.	expel	expels	expelled	expelling
4.	cartel	cartels	propeller	expulsion
5.	impel	impels	impelled	impelling
6.	pastel	pastels	impulse	impulsive
7.	* **Abel**	Abel's	kennel	kennels
8.	Israel	Israel's	Israelis	Israelites
9.	**Michael**	Michael's	Ishmael	**Michael**
10.	**label**	labels	**labeled** labelled	**labeling** labelling
11.	**cancel**	cancels	**canceled** cancelled	**canceling** cancelling
12.	Marcel	Marcel's	cancellation	cancellations
13.	parcel	parcels	**parceled** parcelled	**parceling** parcelling
14.	**model**	models	**modeled** modelled	**modeling** modelling
15.	yodel	yodels	**yodeled** yodelled	**yodeling** yodelling
16.	citadel	citadels	fidelity	Fidel
17.	infidel	infidels	infidelity	infidelities
18.	*** **angel**	angels	angelic	angelically
19.	satchel	satchels	**bushel**	bushels
20.	Ethel	Ethel's	**camel**	camels
21.	**nickel**	nickels	yokel	yokels
22.	**panel**	panels	**paneled** panelled	**paneling** panelling
23.	**channel**	channels	**chaneled** channelled	**chaneling** channelling
24.	**flannel**	flannels	* **kernel**	**kernels**
25.	Lionel	Lionel's	* **colonel**	the **colonel's**

* Homophones:

able/Abel   When Cain's brother was healthy, he was called able Abel.
kernel/colonel   One kernel of corn refused to pop. The colonel threw it out.

** Heteronyms: These particular heteronyms can be spelled without doubling the -l. This is the traditional American way. However, many American writers are following the British tradition and double the -l. Note, that when the -el carries the accent as in compel and dispel the letter l must be doubled regardless of whether you are British or American.

*** Tricky Word: angel ("AY'n jul") Do you have a guardian angel?
                           angle ("ANG gul") Do you know what a right angle is?

	105th day	106th day	107th day	108th day
1.	Col. Brown	Colonel Brown	colonels	colonel
2.	**tunnel**	tunnels	tunneled tunnelled	tunneling tunnelling
3.	funnel	funnels	funneled funnelled	funneling funnelling
4.	shrapnel	sentinel	sentinels	dorsel fin
5.	chapel	chapels	chaplain	chaplains
6.	scalpel	scalpels	gospel	gospels
7.	**barrel**	barrels	barreled barrelled	barreling barrelling
8.	scoundrel	scoundrels	mongrel	mongrels
9.	**quarrel**	quarrels	quarreled quarrelled	quarrelling
10.	squirrel	squirrels	squirreled squirrelled	squirreling squirrelling
11.	wastrel	wastrels	minstrel	minstrels
12.	apparel	doggerel	easel	easels
13.	diesel	diesels	weasel	weasels
14.	chisel	chisels	chiseled chiselled	chiseling chiselling
15.	damsel	damsels	tinsel	counselor counsellor
16.	morsel	morsels	tassel	tassels
17.	vessel	vessels	sequel	sequels
18.	marvel	marvels	**marvelous**	marvelously
19.	**jewel**	jewels	jeweler	jewelry
20.	**towel**	towels	trowel	trowels
21.	vowel	vowels	pretzels	mazel tov
22.	* **counsel**	counsels	counseled counselled	counseling counselling
23.	* **council**	councils	councilor councillor	councilors councillors
24.	**pencil**	pencils	pupil	pupils
25.	stencil	stencils	vigil	vigils

* Homophones:

counsel/council   The lawyer had to counsel the city council.

	109th day	110th day	111th day	112th day
1.	peril	perils	perilous	perilously
2.	imperil	imperils	imperiled imperilled	imperiling imperilling
3.	**April**	April's rains	tonsil	tonsils
4.	utensil	utensils	fossil	fossils
5.	**evil**	evils	boll weevil	weevils
6.	**devil**	devils	daffodil	daffodils
7.	bedevil	bedevils	bedeviled bedevilled	bedeviling bedevilling
8.	civil	uncivil	civilian	civilians
9.	civilize	civilized	civilization	civility
10.	Virgil	Brazil	jonquil	jonquils
11.	tranquil	tranquilize tranquilise	tranquilizer tranquiliser	tranquility
12.	**owl**	owls	jowl	jowls
13.	howl	howls	howled	howling
14.	scowl	scowls	scowled	scowling
15.	growl	growls	growled	growling
16.	prowl	prowls	prowled	prowling
17.	*** fowl**	fowls	prowler	prowlers
18.	*** bowl**	bowls	bowled	bowling
19.	bowler	bowlers	**sugar** bowl	the Rose Bowl
20.	**fuel**	fuels	fueled fuelled	fueling fuelling
21.	refuel	refuels	refueled refuelled	refueling refuelling
22.	*** duel**	duels	dueled duelled	dueling duelling
23.	**cruel**	cruelly	cruelty	**salve**
24.	gruel	grueling gruelling	**usual**	usually
25.	*** dual**	duals	unusual	unusually

* Homophones:

fowl/foul	What do you call a bad-tasting bird? A foul fowl.
bowl/boll	You can have a bowl of cereal or bowl a strike. A boll weevil destroys cotton crops.
duel/dual	What do you call two sets of twins fighting each other? A dual duel.

! Insane Words: sugar ("shuug gur") salve ("SAV").

	113th day	114th day	115th day	116th day
1.	bulb	tulip bulbs	bulb	light bulbs
2.	bald	balding	baldness	bald
3.	scald	scalds	scalded	scalding
4.	Donald	Donald's	McDonald	McDonald's
5.	Ronald	Ronald	MacDonald	MacDonald's
6.	**field**	fields	fielded	fielding
7.	fielder	fielders	infield	outfield
8.	infielder	infielders	outfielder	outfielders
9.	wield	wields	wielded	wielding
10.	yield	yields	yielded	yielding
11.	shield	shields	shielded	shielding
12.	windshield	windshields	builder	builders
13.	* **build**	builds	**built**	**building**
14.	gild a lily	gilds	gilt	gilding
15.	guild	guilds	**guilt**	**guilty**
16.	plebe	plebes	plebian	cubing
17.	**tube**	tubes	tubing	cubic
18.	cube	cube	cubes	cubical
19.	**probable**	probably	probability	probabilities
20.	indescribable	indescribably	manageable	unmanageable
21.	readable	unreadable	readability	abilities
22.	commendable	commendably	marriageable	knowledgeable
23.	dependable	dependably	dependability	changeable
24.	expendable	peaceable	peaceably	unchangeable
25.	replaceable	irreplaceable	agreeable	agreeably

* Homophones:
build/billed We like to build bird houses. We don't like to be billed for bird houses.

	117th day	118th day	119th day	120th day
1.	traceable	untraceable	serviceable	likeable
2.	noticeable	noticeably	unenforceable	saleable
3.	sizeable	unspeakable	unreasonable	irreparable
4.	affable	unbreakable	unreasonably	irreparably
5.	indefatigable	unthinkable	unseasonably	innumerable
6.	navigable	remarkable	personable	venerable
7.	teachable	remarkably	capable	vulnerable
8.	unteachable	workable	capability	invulnerable
9.	untouchable	available	capabilities	operable
10.	laughable	unavailable	incapable	inoperable
11.	appreciable	syllable	inescapable	miserable
12.	appreciably	monosyllable	bearable	miserably
13.	sociable	**flammable**	unbearable	admirable
14.	sociably	**inflammable**	parable	admirably
15.	unsociable	attainable	parables	desirable
16.	unsociably	imaginable	separable	undesirable
17.	**society**	unimaginable	inseparable	adorable
18.	**social**	pardonable	** **separate** rooms	deplorable
19.	socially	unpardonable	separately	memorable
20.	anti-social	fashionable	comparable	honorable
21.	liable	fashionably late	comparably	honorably
22.	**reliable**	unfashionable	incomparable	favorable
23.	unreliable	companionable	considerable	favorably
24.	undeniable	impressionable	considerably	honourable
25.	undeniably	questionable	insufferable	favourable

** Heteronyms:
separate adj. ("SEP rit")/separate v. ("SEP uh RAY't")

Synonyms:
The words *flammable* and *inflammable* mean exactly the same! Go figure!

Evaluation Test #3
(After 120 Days)

#	Sentence	Pattern being tested	Lesson word is in
1.	Do you like standing in a rec**eiving** line?	ceiving	84
2.	Most people enjoy going to a wedding rec**eption**.	ception	84
3.	I like people who are ch**eerful**.	eerful	85
4.	They did what they were asked to do ch**eerfully**.	eerfully	86
5.	It's no fun losing your l**uggage** on vacation.	age	87
6.	Sometimes it's necessary to have a strict b**udget**.	udge	89
7.	When was post**age** less than a dime?	age	91
8.	Cattle are sl**aughtered** everyday in stockyards.	aughtered	91
9.	My neighbor enjoys lifting w**eights**.	eights	94
10.	The squ**eaky** wheel gets the grease.	eaky	95
11.	Our motor needs to be overh**auled**.	auled	99
12.	The two reb**els** were caught and tried for treason.	els	98
13.	Not all reb**ellions** are successful.	ellions	99
14.	Some people are very imp**ulsive**.	ulsive	104
15.	I dislike people who are always qu**arreling (quarrelling)**.	arreling*	108
16.	People should act civ**ilized**.	ivilized	110
17.	The pr**owlers** were caught by the police.	owlers	112
18.	The outf**ielders** collided going for the flyball.	ielders	116
19.	They prob**ably** didn't hear each other yell, "It's mine."	obably	114
20.	The mayor was unav**ailable** for comment.	ailable	118

* Both -eling and -elling are correct! But a writer should be consistent. Either all words like quarrel, shovel, tunnel, etc. should take double -l's in the -ed and -ing forms or just single -l's. Single l's are traditionally American spelling. Double l's, British.

Name_____   Date_____

Evaluation Test #3

1. Do you like standing in a rec_____ line?

2. Most people enjoy going to a wedding rec_____.

3. I like people who are ch_____.

4. They did what they were asked to do ch_____.

5. It's no fun losing your l_____ on vacation.

6. Sometimes it's necessary to have a strict b_____.

7. When was post_____ less than a dime?

8. Cattle are sl_____ everyday in stockyards.

9. My neighbor enjoys lifting w_____.

10. The squ_____ wheel gets the grease.

11. Our motor needs to be overh_____.

12. The two reb_____ were caught and tried for treason.

13. Not all reb_____ are successful.

14. Some people are very imp_____.

15. I dislike people who are always qu_____.

16. People should act civ_____.

17. The pr_____ were caught by the police.

18. The outf_____ collided going for the fly ball.

19. They prob_____ didn't hear each other yell, "It's mine."

20. The mayor was unav_____ for comment.

	121st day	122nd day	123rd day	124th day
1.	variable	unquestionably	tolerable	incurable
2.	invariably	reasonable	intolerable	durable
3.	pleasurable	excitable	accountable	believable
4.	measurable	profitable	accountability	unbelievable
5.	immeasurable	profitably	unaccountable	forgivable
6.	advisable	profitability	notable	unforgivable
7.	advisability	unprofitable	notably	livable
8.	inadvisable	imitable	potable	unlivable
9.	indispensable	inimitable	potent potables	lovable
10.	disposable	hospitable	quotable	lovably
11.	passable	inhospitable	adaptable	unlovable
12.	passably	hospitality	adaptability	movable
13.	impassable	hospital	**acceptable**	immovable
14.	usable	charitable	unacceptable	allowable
15.	unusable	charitably	**comfortable**	taxable
16.	excusable	veritable	comfortably	payable
17.	inexcusable	veritably	uncomfortable	unpayable
18.	debatable	**irritable**	**portable**	employable
19.	**respectable**	irritability	detestable	unemployable
20.	respectability	suitable	regrettable	employability
21.	**predictable**	suitably	regrettably	recognizable
22.	predictability	unsuitable	irrefutable	unrecognizable
23.	unpredictable	inevitable	irrefutably	allowable
24.	predictably	inevitability	indisputable	observable
25.	**vegetables**	lamentable	inscrutable	unobservable

	125th day	126th day	127th day	128th day
1.	marketable	presentable	valuable	constable
2.	uninhabitable	unpresentable	invaluable	inconceivable
3.	**Bible**	Bibles	bauble	baubles
4.	noble	nobles	nobility	nobler
5.	feeble	feebler	feeblest	feeble-minded
6.	ruble	rubles	foible	foibles
7.	**double**	doubles	doubled	doubling
8.	**trouble**	troubles	troubled	troubling
9.	**possible**	possibly	possibility	possibilities
10.	**impossible**	impossibly	impossibility	**! salmon**
11.	audible	audibly	audience	auditorium
12.	inaudible	inaudibly	audition	auditory nerves
13.	invincible	invincibly	invincibility	**! psalm**
14.	legible	legibly	legislature	legible
15.	illegible	illegibly	legislation	illegible
16.	forcible	forcibly	legislator	alleged
17.	enforceable	unenforceable	**legal**	allegiance
18.	edible	reducible	**illegal**	sieve
19.	inedible	irreducible	legality	legalities
20.	credible	credibly	credibility	**niece**
21.	incredible	incredibly	sieve	**nephew**
22.	intelligible	intelligibly	intelligent	intelligence
23.	incorrigible	incorrigibly	incorrigibility	incorrigibles
24.	tangible	tangibles	tangibly	tangibility
25.	intangible	intangibles	intangibly	intangibility

! Insane words:

psalm ("SAH'm") has a silent p and a silent l.
salmon ("SAM mun") has a silent l.

	129th day	130th day	131st day	132nd day
1.	indelible	indelibly	neglect	**psalm**
2.	negligible	negligibly	negligent	negligence
3.	fallible	fallibly	fallacy	fallacies
4.	infallible	infallibly	infallibility	fallacious
5.	gullible	gullibly	gullibility	**debts**
6.	discernible	discernibly	discernibility	indebted
7.	indiscernible	indiscernibly	**It's** mediocre.	**They're** mediocre.
8.	**terrible**	terribly	**terror**	terrified
9.	**horrible**	horribly	horror	horrified
10.	feasible	feasibly	feasibility	**There's** no hope.
11.	infeasible	infeasibly	infeasibility	**You're** right.
12.	visible	visibly	visibility	vision
13.	invisible	invisibly	invisibility	visionary
14.	divisible	divisibly	division	divide
15.	indivisible	indivisibly	**They're** nice people.	**We're** going **too**.
16.	defensible	defensibly	defense defence**	defensive defencive**
17.	indefensible	indefensibly	**They're** in **debt**.	**We're** in **debt too**.
18.	reprehensible	reprehensibly	comprehension	comprehensive
19.	comprehensible	comprehensibly	comprehensibility	comprehend
20.	apprehensible	incomprehensibly	apprehend	apprehension
21.	**sensible**	sensibly	sensibility	sensibilities
22.	**responsible**	responsibly	responsibility	responsibilities
23.	irresponsible	irresponsibly	responsive	irresponsible
24.	reversible	reversibly	mediocre	**! mustache**
25.	irreversible	irreversibly	mediocrity	deuce

* Homophones:
defense (American spelling) / defence (British spelling)

! Insane Words: mustache ("MUSS tash")

	133rd day	134th day	135th day	136th day
1.	impassible	impassibly	deuce	deuces
2.	**possible**	**possibly**	**possibility**	**possibilities**
3.	**impossible**	impossibly	impossibility	**! mustache**
4.	accessible	permit	permission	permissive
5.	inaccessible	inaccessibly	inaccessibility	**They're** going, **too**.
6.	irrepressible	irrepressibly	irrepressibility	**It's** too bad.
7.	admissible	inadmissible	admissibility	inadmissibility
8.	permissible	impermissible	permissibility	**We're** going to go.
9.	plausible	implausible	plausibility	implausible
10.	compatible	incompatible	compatibility	incompatibility
11.	destructible	indestructible	indestructibility	indestructible
12.	perceptible	imperceptible	contemptible	susceptible
13.	convertible	convertibles	suggestible	suggestibility
14.	digestible	indigestible	resistible	irresistible
15.	exhaustible	inexhaustible	combustible	combustibles
16.	flexible	inflexible	flexibility	inflexible
17.	babble	babbles	babbled	babbling
18.	babbler	babblers	feud	feuding
19.	rabble	pebble	pebbles	pebbly
20.	scrabble	dribbler	dribblers	**There's too** many **there**.
21.	dribble	dribbles	dribbled	dribbling
22.	nibble	nibbles	nibbled	nibbling
23.	quibble	quibbles	quibbled	quibbling
24.	scribble	scribbles	scribbled	scribbling
25.	scribbler	scribblers	double	trouble

	137th day	138th day	139th day	140th day
1.	gobble	gobbles	gobbled	gobbling
2.	hobble	hobbles	hobbled	hobbling
3.	bobble	bobbles	bobbled	bobbling
4.	cobble	cobbles	cobbled	cobbling
5.	cobbler	cobblers	cobblestone	cobblestones
6.	**bubble**	bubbles	bubbled	bubbling
7.	**double**	doubles	doubled	doubling
8.	**trouble**	troubles	troubled	troubling
9.	stubble	rubble	feuds	feuded
10.	ladle	ladles	ladled	ladling
11.	cradle	cradles	cradled	cradling
12.	needle	needles	needled	needling
13.	tweedle	wheedle	wheedles	wheedling
14.	*** idle**	idles	idled	idling
15.	idly	idler	idol	idolize
16.	bridle	bridles	unbridled	bridal
17.	sidle	sidles	sidled	sidling
18.	boodle	boodles	noodle	noodles
19.	doodle	doodles	doodled	doodling
20.	poodle	poodles	doodler	doodlers
21.	dawdle	dawdles	dawdled	dawdling
22.	pilfer	pilfers	pilfered	pilfering
23.	**golf**	golfs	golfed	golfing
24.	golfer	golfers	wolves	werewolves
25.	wolf	wolfed down	wolfs down	wolfing

* Homophones:

idle/idol   What do you call a lazy god? An idle idol.

	141st day	142nd day	143rd day	144th day
1.	gulf	gulfs	Gulf of Mexico	Persian Gulf
2.	engulf	engulfs	engulfed	engulfing
3.	bulge	bulges	bulged	bulging
4.	indulge	indulges	indulged	indulging
5.	divulge	divulges	divulged	divulging
6.	* caulk	caulks	caulked	caulking
7.	* calk	calks	calked	calking
8.	elk	elks	Dr. Welk	Dr. Welk's
9.	folk	folks	folk song	folk dance
10.	* yolk	yolks	Dr. Polk	Dr. Polk's polka
11.	* yoke	yokes	yoked	yoking
12.	bulk	bulky	bulkier	bulkiest
13.	sulk	sulks	sulked	sulking
14.	skulk	skulks	skulked	skulking
15.	hulk	hulks	feuds	feuded
16.	elm	elms	helm	helms
17.	Elmer	Elmer's tune	helmet	helmets
18.	whelm	whelms	spaghetti	spaghetti
19.	overwhelm	overwhelms	overwhelmed	overwhelming
20.	film	films	filmed	filming
21.	gulp	gulps	gulped	gulping
22.	pulp	pulps	pulpy	pulpit
23.	* false	falsely	false alarm	false alarms
24.	falsehood	falsehoods	false face	false faces
25.	falsify	falsifies	falsified	falsifying

* Homophones:

false/faults — What do you call untrue imperfections? False faults.
caulk/calk — You can caulk a crack or calk a crack, your choice.
yolk/yoke — The center (yellow part) of an egg is the yolk. You can yoke oxen to a plow.

	145th day	146th day	147th day	148th day
1.	or **else**	elsewhere	Elsie	or else
2.	**pulse**	pulses	* choir	convulsive
3.	impulse	impulses	impulsive	impulsively
4.	repulse	repulses	repulsive	convulsion
5.	convulse	convulses	convulsed	convulsing
6.	**salt**	salts	salted	salting
7.	**salty**	saltier	saltiest	Malta
8.	malt	malts	malted milk	Walter Mitty
9.	**halt**	halts	halted	halting
10.	exalt	exalts	exalted	exalting
11.	**fault**	* **faults**	faulted	faulting
12.	faulty	faultier	faultiest	* **choirs**
13.	default	defaults	defaulted	defaulting
14.	pole vault	vaults	vaulted	vaulting
15.	pole-vaulter	pole-vaulters	pole-vaulter	pole-vaulters
16.	pole-vault	pole-vaults	pole-vaulted	pole-vaulting
17.	**assault**	assaults	assaulted	assaulting
18.	somersault	somersaults	somersaulted	somersaulting
19.!	* Sault Ste. Marie	**spelt	shelter	shelters
20.	**belt**	belts	belted	belting
21.	**melt**	melts	melted	melting
22.	smelt	smelts	smelted	smelting
23.	pelt	pelts	pelted	pelting
24.	welt	welts	welter	sweltered
25.	! **dealt**	swelter	swelters	sweltering

* Homophones:

choirs/quires   People sing in choirs. Paper comes in quires.
Sault/Sioux/sue/Soo   People from the Soo (Sault Ste. Marie) have heard of Sioux City Sue.

** Note: In American English, the past tense (-ed form) of the word *spell* is *spelled*. However, in British English the older form (-elt) is used to form *spelt*. Compare feel/felt.

! Insane words:

dealt ("delt")In many "eel" words such as *feel*, the past tense is "elt." The past tense of *deal* ("deel") is *dealt* ("delt").

Sault Ste. Marie ("SOO SAY'n-t muh REE") Normally the abbreviation for the title *Saint* is *St.*, but since these U.S. and Canadian cities were named by the early French explorers, the feminine French abbreviation for *Saint* (*Ste.*) is used. In French, the masculine is St. the feminine, Ste. In Spanish the feminine is Santa (Santa Rosa) and the masculine is San (San Francisco).

	149th day	150th day	151st day	152nd day
1.	**bolt**	bolts	bolted	bolting
2.	unbolt	unbolts	unbolted	unbolting
3.	thunderbolt	thunderbolts	colt	colts
4.	jolt	jolts	jolted	jolting
5.	**volt**	volts	revolution	revolutionary
6.	revolt	revolts	revolted	revolting
7.	**molt**	molts	molted	molting
8.	**moult****	moults	moulted	moulting
9.	**adult**	adults	*** choir**	*** choirs**
10.	**insult**	insults	insulted	insulting
11.	**result**	results	resulted	resulting
12.	consult	consults	consulted	consultation
13.	exult	exults	exulted	exultation
14.	catapult	catapults	catapulted	catapulting
15.	cult	cults	occult	spaghetti
16.	**difficult**	difficulty	difficulties	difficult
17.	waltz	waltzes	waltzed	waltzing
18.	**silver**	silvery	Silver's hoofs	silver
19.	**solve**	solves	solved	solution
20.	dissolve	dissolves	dissolved	dissolution
21.	revolve	revolves	revolved	revolution
22.	absolve	absolves	absolved	absolution
23.	involve	involves	involved	involution
24.	resolve	resolves	resolved	resolution
25.	**! salve**	salves	calves	halves

* Homophones:

molt/moult	Either spelling is correct.
quire/choir	The choir director needed to buy a quire of paper.
acquire/a quire/a choir	What is to gain 500 sheets of paper? To acquire a quire.
	What is to gain a group of singers? To acquire a choir.

! Insane words:

salve ("SAV")	Rhymes with have. The letter l is silent.

	153rd day	154th day	155th day	156th day
1.	**aim**	aims	aimed	aiming
2.	**claim**	claims	claimed	claiming
3.	reclaim	reclaims	reclaimed	** reclamation
4.	acclaim	acclaims	acclaimed	** acclamation
5.	**exclaim**	exclaims	exclaimed	** exclamation
6.	proclaim	proclaims	proclaiming	** proclamation
7.	disclaim	disclaims	disclaimer	disclaimers
8.	maim	maims	maimed	maiming
9.	madam	madams	William	William's
10.	macadam	Gotham City	bedlam	balsam
11.	Islam	Islamic	wigwam	wigwams
12.	**program**	programs	**They're** winning.	**Their** dog died.
13.	* **programme**	** programmes	programmed	programming
14.	anthem	anthems	mayhem	**You're** okay.
15.	emblem	emblems	**It's too** late.	**Your** hat fell off.
16.	**problem**	problems	problematic	problematical
17.	**item**	items	itemize	itemization
18.	totem	totems	**We're** going.	**They're** losing.
19.	**system**	systems	systematic	systematically
20.	solemn	solemnly	solemnity	**Your** cat hurt **its** paw.
21.	**victim**	victims	victimize	**You're** right!
22.	pilgrim	pilgrims	pilgrimage	pilgrimages
23.	denim	blue denims	**You're** all right.	**Your** right hand.
24.	*** seraphim	*** cherubim	*** goyim	**They're** coming.
25.	verbatim	**They're** all right.	**Their** dog died.	**We're** almost **there**.

* Homophones:
program/programme   Americans prefer to program computers. The British programme them.

** Vowel & Accent shift. The long a sound (spelled ai) in the base claim changes to the schwa ("uh") sound spelled by the letter a when we add -ation ("AY shun").

*** Irregular Plural Occasionally we keep the plural endings of words we borrow from other languages. For example, in Latin words ending in –us have the plural i as in one alumnus and many alumni. In these cases, the plural form is from the Hebrew language. One seraph, one cherub, one goy. Many seraphim, cherubim, and goyim.

	157th day	158th day	159th day	160th day
1.	**animal**	animals	animate	animation
2.	decimal	decimals	decimate	decimated
3.	mammal	mammals	They're our friends.	**There** are lots of reasons.
4.	thermal	thermometer	thermometers	They want **their** money.
5.	**formal**	formals	formally	formality
6.	informal	**Their** car is gone.	informally	informality
7.	**normal**	abnormal	normally	abnormality
8.	dismal	dismally	baptismal records	**They're** losing.
9.	to whom?	by whom?	for whom?	against whom?
10.	freedom	freedoms	random	randomly
11.	boredom	seldom	Christendom	martyrdom
12.	**wise**	fathom	fathoms	snake venom
13.	wisdom	idiom	idioms	idiomatic
14.	axiom	axioms	axiomatic	**We're** winning.
15.	pogrom	pogroms	phantom	phantoms
16.	ransom	ransoms	ransomed	ransoming
17.	blossom	blossoms	blossomed	blossoming
18.	**atom**	atoms	atomic	** **aluminum**
19.	**symptom**	symptoms	symptomatic	** **aluminium**
20.	**custom**	customs	customize	customer
21.	**bottom**	bottoms	bottomed	bottoming
22.	museum	museums	calcium	gymnasium
23.	radium	helium	**premium**	premiums
24.	**stadium**	stadiums	uranium	**auditorium**
25.	**medium**	tedium	geranium	geraniums

** **Note:** Americans use the spelling aluminum ("uh LOO min um"); the British use aluminium ("AL yoo MIN ee um"). One glance at the atomic chart with all the metals in one series spelled -ium as in calcium, barium, sodium, magnesium, Lithium, radium, potassium, etc., would indicate the British are eminently correct and that the Americans have perpetuated a misspelling and mispronunciation for such a long that it has become standard American English and hence "correct."

Evaluation Test #4
(After 160 Days)

	Pattern Being Tested	Lesson word is in
1. I just love Southern hospit**ality**.	ality	122
2. I wish you would stop being so irrit**able**.	able	122
3. Your handwriting is absolutely illeg**ible**.	ible	125
4. Your work is incred**ibly** good.	ibly	126
5. We all have different respons**ibilities**.	ilities	132
6. There ought to be room in the program for flex**ibility**.	ility	135
7. Just what is tr**oubling** you?	oubling	140
8. I wish you would stop n**eedling** me.	eedling	140
9. That movie was just absolutely overwh**elming**.	elming	144
10. I would love to hear a rapper sing a f**olk** song.	olk	141
11. Everyone should have a good strong p**ulse**.	ulse	145
12. There's no excuse for **a**ss**aulting** another person.	aulting	148
13. What a rev**olting** development this is.	olting	152
14. Have you ever kept a New Year's res**olution**?	olution	152
15. What's the pr**oblem**?	oblem	153
16. All syst**ems** are go.	tems	154
17. The governor procl**aimed** today as NOW day.	aimed	155
18. That was an official procl**amation**.	amation	156
19. Do you know the sym**ptoms** of pellagra?	ptoms	158
20. They held the school play in the audit**orium**.	orium	160

Name_____Date_____

Evaluation Test #4

1. I just love Southern hospit_____.

2. I wish you would stop being so irrit_____.

3. Your handwriting is absolutely illeg_____.

4. Your work is incred_____ good.

5. We all have different respons_____ .

6. There ought to be room in the program for flex_____ .

7. Just what is tr_____ you?

8. I wish you would stop n_____ me.

9. That movie was just absolutely overwh_____.

10. I would love to hear a rapper sing a f_____ song.

11. Everyone should have a good strong p_____.

12. There's no excuse for ss_____ another person.

13. What a rev_____ development this is.

14. Have you ever kept a New Year's res_____ ?

15. What's the pr_____ ?

16. All syst_____ are go.

17. The governor procl_____ today as NOW day.

18. That was an official procl_____ .

19. Do you know the sym_____ of pellagra?

20. They held the school play in the audit_____ .

	161st day	162nd day	163rd day	164th day
1.	potassium	planetarium	solarium	barium
2.	titanium	Belgium	aquarium	delirium
3.	magnesium	symposium	emporium	sanitarium
4.	amber	ambergris	somber	somberly
5.	ember	embers	September	September's child
6.	**member**	members	November	November's child
7.	**remember**	**remembers**	**remembered**	remembering
8.	dismember	dismembers	dismembered	dismembering
9.	limber	limbers	limbered	limbering
10.	timber	timbers	timbered	timbering
11.	lumber	lumbers	lumbered	lumbering
12.	slumber	slumbers	slumbered	slumbering
13.	**number**	numbers	numbered	numbering
14.	misnumber	misnumbers	misnumbered	misnumbering
15.	encumber	encumbers	encumbered	encumbering
16.	**cucumber**	cucumbers	chamber	chambers
17.	amble	ambles	ambled	ambling
18.	ramble	rambles	rambled	rambling
19.	gamble	gambles	gambled	gambling
20.	gambler	gamblers	rambler	ramblers
21.	scramble	scrambles	scrambled eggs	scrambling
22.	scrambler	scramblers	shambles	nimble
23.	tremble	trembles	trembled	trembling
24.	assemble	assembled	**assembly**	assemblies
25.	disassemble	disassembles	disassembled	disassembling

	165th day	166th day	167th day	168th day
1.	resemble	resembles	resembling	resemblance
2.	thimble	thimbles	Wimbledon	nimbly
3.	humble	humbles	humbled	humbling
4.	**tumble**	tumbles	tumbled	tumbling
5.	**stumble**	stumbles	stumbled	stumbling
6.	jumble	jumbles	jumbled	jumbling
7.	**fumble**	fumbles	fumbled	fumbling
8.	**mumble**	mumbles	mumbled	mumbling
9.	rumble	rumbles	rumbled	rumbling
10.	**grumble**	grumbles	grumbled	grumbling
11.	**theme**	themes	**supreme**	supremely
12.	scheme	schemes	schemed	scheming
13.	**extreme**	extremes	extremity	extremities
14.	**extremely**	unassuming	assumption	assumptions
15.	**assume**	assumes	assumed	assuming
16.	costume	costumes	costumed	costuming
17.	consume	consumes	consumed	consuming
18.	consumer	consumers	consumption	presumption
19.	presume	presumes	presumed	presuming
20.	** **resume**	resumes	resumed	resuming
21.	plume	plumes	resumption	gumption
22.	fume	fumes	fumed	fuming
23.	**perfume**	perfumes	ghetto	ghettos
24.	**empty**	empties	emptied	emptying
25.	Humpty	Humpty Dumpty	H. Dumpty's fall	spaghetti

**** Heteronyms:**

resume/resumé To begin again is to resume ("ree ZOOM"). To make a list of all your jobs and positions is to write your resumé ("REZ zuh MAY").

	169th day	170th day	171st day	172nd day
1.	hemp	Kemp	temp	choirboy
2.	**temper**	tempers	tempered	tempering
3.	temperature	temperatures	distemper	chorus
4.	tamper	tampers	tampered	tampering
5.	**camper**	campers	damper	dampers
6.	pamper	**pampers**	**pampered**	pampering
7.	whimper	whimpers	whimpered	whimpering
8.	simper	simpers	simpered	simpering
9.	romper	rompers	**bumper**	bumpers
10.	**jumper**	jumpers	plumper	Thumper
11.	ample	amply	example	examples
12.	**sample**	samples	sampled	sampling
13.	trample	tramples	trampled	trampling
14.	**temple**	temples	sampler	samplers
15.	**simple**	simpler	simplest	simply
16.	**pimple**	pimples	pimpled	pimply
17.	**dimple**	dimples	dimpled	dimpling
18.	rumple	rumples	rumpled	rumpling
19.	**crumple**	crumples	crumpled	crumpling
20.	**again**	again and again	against	up against it
21.	**mountain**	mountains	mountainous	conquer
22.	**fountain**	fountains	uncertain	unconquered
23.	**certain**	certainly	certainty	uncertainty
24.	villain	villains	villainous	villainously
25.	**bargain**	bargains	bargained	bargaining

68

	173rd day	174th day	175th day	176th day
1.	**captain**	captains	captained	captaining
2.	**curtain**	curtains	Britain	Britain's economy
3.	urban	suburban	interurban	Dominican
4.	turban	turbans	Michael Jordan	conqueror
5.	Mohican	Mohicans	pagan	pagans
6.	publican	publicans	slogan	slogans
7.	**Republican**	Republicans	toboggan	toboggans
8.	pelican	pelicans	cardigan	cardigans
9.	Anglican	Anglicans	organ	organs
10.	**American**	Americans	Gilligan	Gilligan's Island
11.	**African**	Africans	Jonathan	Jonathan's
12.	**Mexican**	Mexicans	veteran	veterans
13.	**Canadian**	Canadians	Texan	Texans
14.	**ocean**	oceans	Atlantic Ocean	Pacific Ocean
15.	Arab	Arabia	Arabian	Arabic
16.	* **Colombia**	Colombian	library	librarian
17.	* **Columbia**	Italy	Italian	Italians
18.	median	medians	vegetarian	vegetarians
19.	comedian	comedians	history	historian
20.	**Indian**	Indians	Indiana	Indiana's Indians
21.	**Australian**	Australians	college	collegian
22.	veterinarian	veterinarians	ruffian	ruffians
23.	Mongol	Mongolia	Mongolian	Mongolians
24.	**Christ**	**Christmas**	**Christian**	**Christianity**
25.	Norway	Norwegian	theology	theologian

* Homophones:

Colombia/Columbia   Washington, D.C. is the District of Columbia. We get a lot of coffee from Colombia.

	177th day	178th day	179th day	180th day
1.	**magic**	**magician**	magicians	magically
2.	logic	logician	logicians	logically
3.	Phoenicia	Phoenician	Phoenicians	**They're too** much.
4.	technical	technician	technicians	technically
5.	**electric**	**electrician**	electricians	electrically
6.	obstetrics	obstetrician	obstetricians	**You're** going **too**?
7.	**music**	**musician**	musicians	musically
8.	physic	**physician**	physicians	physically
9.	arithmetic	arithmetician	arithmeticians	arithmetically
10.	**politics**	**politician**	politicians	politically
11.	optic	optician	opticians	optically
12.	statistic	statistician	statisticians	statistically
13.	Confucius	Confucian	Confucians	**We're** not feuding.
14.	**Asia**	**Asian**	Asians	Asiatic
15.	Caucasus	Caucasian	Caucasians	chorus
16.	Eurasia	Eurasian	Eurasians	* **chords**
17.	Paris	Parisian	Parisians	**Their** cat chased our dog.
18.	Persia	Persian	Persians	**It's** almost time.
19.	Russia	Russian	Russians	**That's too** bad.
20.	Prussia	Prussian	Prussians	old-fashioned
21.	**issue**	issues	issued	Issuing
22.	**tissue**	tissues	cushion	cushions
23.	fashion	fashions	fashioned	fashioning
24.	**Jose** Gonzales	**Jesus** Gonzales	**Jose** Gonzales	**Jesus** Gonzales
25.	**frijoles**	frijoles	frijoles	frijoles

* Homophones:

chords/cords   Musicians play with chords. Woodsmen work with cords of wood.

* "FANCY" Words:

Jose / Jesus / frijoles   In Spanish, the letter J is pronounced as an H, so Jose is pronounced "HO ZAY" and Jesus is pronounced "HAY ZOO-ss" and frijoles is pronounced "free HO layz."

issue / tissue   In these words the letters ss have the sound of /sh/.

70

FINAL EVALUATION TEST

		Pattern being tested	Lesson word is in
1.	We have some unfin**ished** business to attend to.	ished	4
2.	Actors just love appl**ause**.	ause	20
3.	Famil**iarity** breeds contempt.	arity	18
4.	My older sister is an electri**cian**.	cian	24
5.	AVKO spe**cial**izes in helping people learn.	cial	34
6.	Do you like previews of coming attr**actions**?	actions	48
7.	How many of the psychic's pre**dictions** came true?	dictions	60
8.	How do you think I arrived at that concl**usion**?	usion	68
9.	We gave them new sw**eaters** for their anniversary.	eaters	80
10.	My sister works for a constr**uction** company.	uction	64
11.	Do you like standing in a re**ceiving** line?	ceiving	84
12.	Most people enjoy going to a wedding re**ception**.	ception	84
13.	Cattle are sl**aughtered** everyday in stockyards.	aughtered	91
14.	Some people are very imp**ulsive**.	ulsive	104
15.	The mayor was unav**ailable** for comment.	ailable	118
16.	I just love Southern hospit**ality**.	ality	122
17.	We all have different respons**ibilities**.	ilities	132
18.	Have you ever kept a New Year's resol**ution**?	olution	152
19.	The governor procl**aimed** today as NOW day.	aimed	155
20.	That was an official procl**amation**.	amation	156
21.	Have you re**membered** everything I've taught you?	membered	163
22.	Never eat scr**ambled** eggs that have turned green.	ambled	163
23.	Be careful when making an ass**umption** about anything.	umption	167
24.	I hate to hear a dog wh**impering**.	impering	172
25.	I have a friend who has become a veget**arian**.	arian	175

Name_____ Date_____

Final Evaluation Test

1. We have some unfin_____ business to attend to.
2. Actors just love appl_____.
3. Famil_____ breeds contempt.
4. My older sister is an electri_____.
5. AVKO spe_____izes in helping people learn.
6. Do you like previews of coming attr_____?
7. How many of the psychic's pre_____ came true?
8. How do you think I arrived at that concl_____?
9. We gave them new sw_____ for their anniversary.
10. My sister works for a constr_____ company.
11. Do you like standing in a re_____ line?
12. Most people enjoy going to a wedding re_____.
13. Cattle are sl_____ everyday in stockyards.
14. Some people are very imp_____.
15. The mayor was unav_____ for comment.
16. I just love Southern hospit_____.
17. We all have different respons_____.
18. Have you ever kept a New Year's resol_____?
19. The governor procl_____ today as NOW day.
20. That was an official procl_____.
21. Have you re_____ everything I've taught you?
22. Never eat scr_____ eggs that have turned green.
23. Be careful when making an ass_____ about anything.
24. I hate to hear a dog wh_____.
25. I have a friend who has become a veget_____.